MEGA-
results

Commercial Real Estate

A Blueprint for Success

MEGA-PRODUCER
results in
Commercial Real Estate

A Blueprint for Success

Robert L. Herd
CRB, CRS, GRI

Mega-Producer Results in Commercial Real Estate: A Blueprint for Success
Robert L. Herd

VP/Editor-in-Chief: Dave Shaut

Executive Editor: Scott Pearson

Associate Acquisitions Editor: Sara Glassmeyer

Developmental Editor: Arlin Kauffman, LEAP Publishing Services, Inc.

Editorial Assistant: Adele Scholtz

Content Project Manager: Elycia Arendt

Sr. Marketing Manager: Mark Linton

Sr. Marketing Communications Manager: Jim Overly

Sr.Technology Project Editor: Matt McKinney

Sr. Manufacturing Coordinator: Charlene Taylor

Art Director: Linda Helcher

Cover and Internal Designer: C Miller Design

Production House: ICC Macmillan Inc.

© 2008 Oncourse Learning

For product information and technology assistance, contact us at
OnCourse Learning & Sales Support, 1-855-733-7239.

For permission to use material from this text or product.

Library of Congress Control Number: 2007924451

ISBN-13: 978-0-324-31409-0

ISBN-10: 0-324-31409-4

OnCourse Learning
3100 Cumberland Blvd Suite 1450
Atlanta, GA 30339
USA

Printed in the United States of America
4 5 6 7 14

Contents

Contents

Contents

Contents

"I'm in commercial real estate."

You have probably heard someone say those words with a great deal of pride in their voice at some type of function, especially real estate industry gatherings.

There is a hierarchy in the real estate industry, mostly unspoken, that puts the commercial real estate agent at the "top of the heap," so to speak. The common belief among many, if not most, residential real estate agents is that the commercial agents sell all the big properties and reap all of the huge commissions, and "Gee, they've gotta be so smart to know all that tax and financial stuff."

There is a lot of truth to such impressions, but there are some major differences between residential and commercial real estate brokerage practices that need to be evaluated carefully before one steps into the commercial arena.

If you really learn your craft, as I did back in the early 1970s, and keep current on the commercial market, it can be the source of many interesting and fun transactions and some very large commissions. However, depending on how you choose to enter the commercial arena, it can also be the source of frustration and financial problems, so you have to be very careful how you go about it.

So how does one get started in commercial real estate, and once started, how does one succeed in building a career that can possibly mean annual sales of $40,000,000 to well over $100,000,000?

This book is a working blueprint for successfully entering or transitioning into commercial real estate, so read on and find out!

Acknowledgments

I would like to dedicate this book to Clyde Rogers.
Although he passed on several years ago, he left a legacy
of trust, commitment, caring, and sharing with his clients
and fellow commercial brokers that still shines like a beacon for all to
aspire to. He was a very special guy.

His patience in mentoring me and teaching me the right way to conduct myself as a commercial broker are appreciated beyond words and will never be forgotten.

P A R T

1

All About Commercial Real Estate

1

Getting Started—It's Decision Time

*C*ommercial real estate is as fast-moving and ever-changing as residential real estate is. That's a fact of life, so if you are going to sell commercial real estate, you owe it to yourself and the clients that you represent to do it right—right from the start.

Listing and selling commercial real estate with a high degree of competency and truly representing the clients who rely on you for commercial services in a professional manner takes a lot of time and knowledge; it isn't simply something that you can dabble in.

Representing the clients who rely on you for commercial services in a professional manner takes a lot of time and knowledge; it isn't simply something that you can dabble in.

Most of the time, the properties you will deal in will be far more expensive than a residential property with many more issues to consider, and there may be extensive tax and/or legal consequences to your client if you don't do each transaction exactly the right way. Simply put, the risks are larger, and the rewards are larger.

Two types of people enter the field of commercial real estate. They are the experienced residential real estate agent and the newly licensed real estate agent.

Experienced residential real estate agents usually start listing and selling commercial real estate because they wish to have more overall knowledge about the other areas of real estate. They also want the ability to better represent their clients in a full-service spectrum of their real estate needs and, of course, the lure of large, even very large, commission checks is always a factor.

Newly licensed real estate agents who enter commercial real estate are most often seniors at or recent graduates of a university with a degree in real estate. They are often sought out by the large commercial firms like Coldwell Banker Commercial, CB Richard Ellis, and Marcus & Millichap Commercial Brokerage. Sometimes they start on some type of an apprentice program where they are paid a small salary and assigned to a senior agent for up to two years, although this practice is fading fast.

So, what's the difference between the two types of people? Basically, it is two things: the amount of commercial real estate knowledge they have, and their ability to stay the course financially until they start closing commercial escrows.

Nearly all of the universities that have degrees in real estate teach a great deal about commercial real estate as a normal part of their curriculum. This gives the college graduate with that kind of degree a real edge in understanding how commercial real estate works as an investment and income-producing tool.

The residential agent seeking that same advantage would do well to start taking the courses that are available through the National Association of REALTORS® that lead to receipt of the professional designation of Certified Commercial Investment Member (CCIM). I'll talk more about that in Chapter 3.

It is very common for experienced as well as new real estate agents who start with a commercial brokerage firm to go as much as one year or more before they actually see any commission checks. If agents affiliate with that type of firm and are not placed on some type of apprenticeship program where they draw a small salary while they get up to speed and build a client base, they had better have a working spouse, a sizeable savings account, or other means of paying their bills.

Agents who maintain their position as a residential salesperson and start to methodically grow their commercial business have the advantage of maintaining the income that they receive through the residential commissions until they start to close commercial transactions, but the complete transition may take considerably longer.

I have counseled many residential agents over the years about how to transition from residential to commercial sales by *time blocking*. What I tell them is to block out 10 percent of their time in their appointment book or daily scheduler to devote to commercial real estate activities, including education, as necessary. Once they completely fill up that amount of time with productive activities, I tell them to increase the time spent on those activities from 10 to 15 percent and just keep increasing it incrementally until they are spending as much time on commercial real estate activities as they wish to, which could be a full-time transition and an exit from residential real estate.

Which is the best way for you to enter the field of commercial real estate? Should you do residential and commercial at the same time or go to work for a commercial firm? It is really a personal decision that will be unique to each person who reads this book. Your finances and your current income from and enjoyment of the residential real estate market will certainly be deciding factors. If you are married, spousal support of what you are doing will be a major factor.

The advantages of going with a commercial real estate firm are numerous, including excellent training programs, a higher degree of credibility to your commercial clients, the high probability of working on larger, more expensive properties that generate larger commission checks, and the vast amount of property and client research that is available to you from the support staff at such firms.

The obvious drawbacks are that it takes longer to research who the contact person is for the larger properties as most are owned by limited liability companies (LLCs), corporations, and other types of entities and finding a "real person" to add to your prospect list can take hours of research, although the emergence of CoStar as a contact source has changed this considerably.

As you will be working on very large properties, the "authorized signatory" for a given property, who often has to report to a committee of some sort, is more cautious about starting a relationship with you and probably won't work with you as soon as residential clients will. You should plan on spending hours a day prospecting for many months to build a client base before you earn a dime.

If you are an experienced residential real estate agent with an existing client base and you go to work at a commercial firm, you will be required to give up your client base except for their commercial real estate needs, and you will have to refer them to a residential agent. I know from experience that each residential transaction that you have to refer to someone else, especially with an old established client, will tear at your heartstrings, so be prepared for it.

I know from experience that each residential transaction that you have to refer to someone else, especially with an old established client, will tear at your heartstrings, so be prepared for it.

If you elect to stay at or join a residential firm and build your commercial base as you do residential, the advantages to you are that you will continue to earn commission checks from your residential activities while you are building a commercial client base. Depending on the policies of the company you work for, you may find that you are referred many commercial clients by the residential agents that are not trained in commercial real estate. This is the case at the company I work for.

Our company's former owner, Paul Lindsey, whom you will meet in Chapter 12 of this book, owned his own commercial real estate firm for over twenty years. He is a CCIM and a very astute commercial broker. He periodically gives classes to a select group of agents within the company who want to do commercial real estate. If they pass his test, they become one of only a small handful of agents in each of the company's offices that are allowed to do commercial transactions. This approach is often very lucrative for them as they have a built-in referral base of eighty to over one hundred agents referring commercial business to them, and they may still do residential transactions as well.

The drawbacks to entering commercial real estate that way are the credibility issue, as stated earlier; the lack of available research resources; and the lack of knowledge and availability of information of what commercial property inventory is currently on the market, as the bigger firms do not always readily share this information, and there is no commercial real estate Multiple Listing Service. The emergence of CoStar and its huge database of commercial properties, which may include currently for sale properties, is changing the landscape somewhat in regard to available inventory.

Let's say that you decide that you want to jump right into a full-time career in commercial real estate, and you are going to need a nest egg to see you through. Where do you find the money? First, be sure that you are totally dedicated to this venture and that you are willing to do everything that it takes to succeed, including working long hours every day and spending countless hours prospecting for new clients.

If you are that dedicated, then there are several options available to you to find the money to give you the financial staying power that you will most certainly need. Just be sure to sit down and do a very careful budget first to see how much money you will really need. This should also include looking for ways to trim your expenses as much as you can.

First, carefully analyze your *true* monthly expenses. Include everything! Then assess what income is available to you each month. This could include a spouse's income, alimony, cash flow from investments you own, dividends, and so forth. Deduct your expenses from your cash flow, and you will have a pretty accurate look at how much cash you will need each month until you cash that first commission check from a commercial transaction. Consider these options:

Savings. There is nothing better than having plenty of cold hard cash in the bank to draw on while you are in your start-up mode. If you are already in real estate sales or have another job that produces excess cash above your expenses every month, there is nothing wrong with saving for a few extra months until you have a year's worth of savings in the bank before you make the change. You'll sleep better at night!

Retirement plans. While many people have large amounts of money in these plans, the money is not easily drawn out without large penalties, and you are basically robbing your future for your present unless you replace it, so drawing on this type of asset should be a last resort.

Home equity. There are two methods of removing equity from your home: a total refinance of your existing loan or a new second loan or equity line of credit. If your existing first loan has an unattractive interest rate, then you may want to consider refinancing it and pulling out the additional cash that you will need to get you through the next year. Be sure to include ten to twelve payments on your new loan if you can. If your first loan is already very large or has an attractive interest rate, then it would probably be wise to leave it alone and get a new second loan or equity line of credit loan.

Borrowing from friends or relatives. As far as I am concerned, this option is off-limits. While it may seem all right at first, it could, and often is, a sure way to create bad feelings in the family or to lose a friend. Please just avoid it if you can. If that is the only cash available to you at the time, then you are probably not a good candidate to enter commercial real estate full-time right now.

Selling assets. Do you have an expensive car with a big payment that you can sell or get out of the lease? It's wise to do so and get something less expensive, at least for now. Do you have a recreational vehicle, boat, or camper in your driveway that you seldom use? If you have any equity in those types of things at all, sell them and bank the cash. Go on, do it! It's your future that you're talking about; and if you do this right, you can buy a bigger, better one later, or you could invest it in real estate for your retirement.

2

Why Commercial Instead of Residential Real Estate?

Soon after I entered the real estate business as a residential agent in 1972, I became very intrigued by commercial real estate and how it worked as an investment, tax shelter, and cash-generating vehicle. I was very fortunate that the broker I worked for rented a room in his office to a very experienced commercial real estate agent named Clyde Rogers. I was very young at the time and full of questions, and, fortunately for me, Clyde was very fatherly and gave freely of his time and his knowledge.

He shared a wealth of information with me about the various types of commercial real estate. I contacted every place I could think of to get books to read about how to successfully list and sell commercial real estate. While I was busy becoming a megaproducer residential agent, I started building a client base of commercial clients that would turn out to be a virtual fun-filled gold mine!

Although Clyde passed on several years ago, I think of him often and thank him to this day.

I always enjoyed the "thrill of the chase" of selling residential real estate, and it produced a very high income for me (so did managing a residential office, which is my true love in the real estate business). I have always been intrigued by the art of matching an investor with just the right income property to meet his or her tax shelter, cash flow, or estate building needs. It's just plain fun and very rewarding, financially and otherwise.

Because of how I started and the success I enjoyed, I personally found it most rewarding to do both commercial and residential real estate at the same time, but I must admit that, looking back over the past thirty-four years, I often wonder about where life would have taken me if I had made the switch to a commercial firm back in the 1970s.

When my wife and I made the move to Arizona in 1999, I was asked to join one of the large commercial brokerage firms in Phoenix, where I specialized in retail shopping centers. It was a very interesting and rewarding experience. I must say that their training, which even veteran agents like me must attend, was very thorough and fully prepares one to conduct business at a highly professional level and with great skill.

It was only the love of managing a real estate office that took me away from it when I was offered the position of branch manager of the flagship office of Tucson's oldest real estate firm—a decision that I have not regretted.

But what about you—why should you enter the world of commercial real estate instead of residential?

It seems that the most talked-about reasons for working in commercial real estate are less weekend work, bigger commissions, and the opportunity to work with people who make decisions based much more on return on investment than emotion, although that's not always true!

While it is true that you will seldom, if ever, work a Sunday in commercial real estate, you will certainly work many Saturdays, and you had better plan on working at least ten hours a day during the week for the first two to three years until you get an established and repeat client base. This is especially true if you work for a large commercial firm because they are numbers-based and performance-oriented and will expect results sooner that later.

Many, if not most residential firms tend to be much more relaxed about performance standards than the commercial firms are and will not watch your performance and daily activities nearly as much as a commercial firm will. It can be uncomfortable, especially if you are not fond of cold calling. However, the increased scrutiny and higher performance standards will also tend to make you more self-disciplined about your time management and the effectiveness of your activities.

Although the vast majority of your work will be conducted during the week, Saturday and even an occasional Sunday are when some of the individual private investors wish to get together to sign listings, hear listing proposals, and listen to offers on their properties.

If you are working on larger investments, the majority of the people whom you work with are only available during the week, so there is minimal weekend work, except for research, cold-calling individual property owners, preparing property brochures and listing proposals, and other tasks.

Smaller NNN investments (in which the tenant pays all of the property's operating expenses, including taxes, insurance, and maintenance) such as fast-food restaurants (the land and building, not the business), Midas Muffler shops, and investments of that nature are often owned by individuals and not by a formal corporate entity, so the owners are usually easier to get in contact with.

While it is true that nearly all residential purchases are based on emotional fulfillment, it is incorrect to think that all commercial purchases are numbers-based or purchased only by a property's return on investment.

It is true that the return on investment is the overwhelming deciding factor almost all of the time; however, resale value, location, and pride of ownership are still factors in many commercial property purchases. The exception to this is the Real Estate Investment Trusts (REITs), which make nearly all of their decisions based on the return on investment (ROI). As an example, one of the ugliest and most forlorn retail shopping centers I had any involvement in was in Apache Junction, Arizona. I had come to know the acquisitions manager of a Texas-based REIT, and he was very happy with this center, even though he had never seen it. It was only when the major tenant decided not to renew the lease on 36,000 square feet that he began to take a more personal interest.

When I sent him some digital pictures, he was less than impressed and began to talk exit strategy with me. I knew that the Salvation Army was looking for about that much space, and I put them in contact with each other. I thought that I might have lost the listing if they leased the space, but that center was so barren and plain ugly that the REIT decided to go ahead with a sale anyway.

Ultimately, you will have to make two major decisions. The first is which type of person or entity you want to work with. What makes you want to get up and go to work more every day? Seeing a buyer get very excited about that special home, or hearing an investor tell you "Yes, this property gives me the return that I want and meets my needs; you've done a great job and I'd like to buy it"?

What makes you want to get up and go to work every day?

The second decision is, if you are sincerely interested in pursuing a career in commercial real estate, how are you going to approach it so that you don't go broke before you get yourself to where you are earning sufficient commissions on a regular basis to maintain yourself and prosper?

I purposely left these two questions for last because I would really like for you to go back and read the first two chapters again, so that you are very clear on what the upside and downside issues of getting into commercial real estate really are. It is work, just like residential real estate is. There is less weekend work. Commissions can be much larger but are more elusive, and escrows can tend to cancel far easier than residential transactions do. You will absolutely need to prospect for hours on end for a long time if you ever want to build a commercial real estate client base.

If, after considering all of these issues, you still want to get into commercial real estate, then it's time to learn what it is all about, so let's get to chapter 3.

3

Train Yourself Thoroughly: Learn! Learn! Learn!

*A*s I told you in Chapter 2, I was very fortunate to have had a mentor early on in my career who taught me a great deal about commercial real estate, but the most important thing he taught me was to never stop learning. This is true about the entire real estate industry, but it is even more critical in commercial real estate because of the size and complexity of many of the transactions, the responsibilities that you take on as an agent, and the inherent potential risks that are a normal part of every commercial transaction, both for you as a practitioner and for your clients.

You might be asking yourself, "What types of risks is he talking about?" Let me give you an example. In the mid-1990s, I came across an ad in the newspaper for a retail shopping center that a well-known residential agent was advertising. I called her and asked if she was cooperating with other agents and if she would send me a marketing package (better known as a "setup"). She sent it to me, and I immediately noticed that there was a gas station on the site. There was no mention of any environmental surveys having been conducted, so I called her and asked her if she or her seller had done a Phase 1 environmental survey. She didn't have a clue about what I was talking about. If an unskilled agent had represented the buyer, the buyer would have inherited a shopping center with two leaking gasoline tanks on the premises and may have been involved in an environmental cleanup that would have cost him over $1,000,000.

If an unskilled agent had represented the buyer, the buyer would have inherited a shopping center with two leaking gasoline tanks on the premises.

In actuality, if a lender is involved, they will most certainly require anywhere from a Phase 1 to a Phase 3 environmental survey, depending on what they find, before they will make a loan on a property that contains any sort of hydrocarbons on site.

The point is that a lack of education could have been a disaster for several people and was certainly an embarrassment to a very good residential agent who had decided to work outside her field of expertise. Don't let that happen to you!

Just as a top residential agent would never even think of going on a listing appointment without doing a very detailed comparative market analysis, a good commercial agent would never think about representing an owner without knowing exactly what is necessary to promote and protect the client's interests.

A good commercial agent would never think about representing an owner without knowing exactly what is necessary to promote and protect the client's interests.

Where can one go to get the information necessary to be fully informed on all aspects of the various types of commercial real estate? There are actually many sources; however, the three best are a well-informed mentor, like I had; the courses that lead to the Certified Commercial Investment Member (CCIM) designation from the National Association of REALTORS®; and in-house training from one of the large commercial brokerage firms. Many good books and CDs are also available from your local, state, and national real estate associations.

If you decide on a career in commercial real estate and are fortunate enough to have a mentor, do whatever it takes to soak up every word that this wonderful person is willing to share with you—especially war stories, as they tend to put learning in context by giving you not only fact-based knowledge but "applied knowledge" as it actually happened in the real world and with real or potential the consequences.

Take your mentor to lunch; shadow him or her if they will allow it; and ask what books, CDs, or tapes you can purchase in order to learn as much as you possibly can. If your mentor could use a part-time assistant, and you have some spare time, think about helping out. You can even do this while you are selling residential real estate for a time.

The CCIM designation is, to me, the working equivalent of having an MBA and going into business management. The courses are not easy by any means, but when you are finished with them, you are so far above and beyond the capabilities of the average commercial real estate agent that there is simply no way to make a valid comparison. It's much like comparing the skills of a CPA to a bookkeeper.

You will crunch numbers for an entire week until you know discounted cash flow analysis and net-present value of future income streams in your sleep. You will learn more about taxation, and its effect on the pre- and after-tax returns achieved by any type of investment property, than you ever thought possible, including how and when to use a tax-deferred exchange to get your client an interest-free loan from the government.

You will learn every method of property value evaluation, including the market data approach to value, the capitalization of net operating income approach to value, how to determine what the internal rate of return of a property is to a given investor, and when and how to use gross rent multipliers to value a property.

Just when you think that you know it all, you will be taught how to conduct a detailed and well-documented site analysis and feasibility study for any kind of investment property.

Remember what it is that we sell as real estate agents: it's not property—the sellers sell property. We sell our time and our knowledge to people who want to buy or sell real estate. In my opinion, there simply is no better way to fine-tune your engine for maximum performance in producing an income, and being able to give top-rated representation to your clients, than to get the CCIM designation.

There simply is no better way to fine-tune your engine for maximum performance in producing an income, and being able to give top-rated representation to your clients, than to get the CCIM designation.

I was so enamored with real estate office management and residential sales that, although I became a CCIM candidate in 1987, I never took the fifth course or did the follow-up work required to get the designation. I still regret it from time to time; I hope you don't do what I did.

If you go to work for one of the large commercial firms, plan on going through some very stringent training. In fact, if you don't have, at the very minimum, a good working knowledge of commercial real estate, and in most cases at least a fair amount of transactional experience, they probably won't even hire you, except for an intern job.

Some of the midsized commercial firms will hire residential agents who seem to "sparkle," although it is very common for those types of firms to be much more into commercial property management and leasing than investment property sales. They always have an investment division, but it is often a minor part of the scope of their operation. If you interview with these types of firms, be sure to ask detailed questions about their training, the scope of the position that you are being considered for, the amount of support that is available to members of the investment division, and what their market share in the investment marketplace has been for the past couple of years.

Your interests will be best served by affiliating with a commercial firm that feels like a good fit and staying there for a long time while you build a loyal client base and gain credibility in the local marketplace, so take your time and interview thoroughly before deciding which one to join.

Your credibility will also be greatly enhanced by attaining a saturation knowledge about and specializing in only one type of commercial real estate investment. You will learn more about this in the next chapter.

4

The Advantages of Specialization

O nce you have affiliated with a commercial firm or decided to stay with your residential real estate firm and make a slow transition to commercial sales, your next step will be to decide whether you will be a jack-of-all-trades type of commercial agent or whether you will specialize in one type of investment only.

If you go to work at almost any of the large commercial real estate firms, then your decision will be made for you. You will be hired to fill a vacancy in one of the specialized areas, such as retail shopping centers, residential income properties, office buildings, ministorages, mobile home parks, hotels, land, and so forth.

If you stay at your residential company, then you call the shots, but be careful! It is an easy mistake to make to try to be "all things to all people," as you won't want to miss out on any possible listings or buyers. However, your interests, and those of your clients, are best served if you narrow your marketing and sales efforts to only one or two types of commercial investments, preferably only one.

If you stay at your residential company, then you call the shots, but be careful! It is an easy mistake to make to try to be "all things to all people."

This gives you the opportunity to go "narrow and deep" in your quest for saturation knowledge about this type of investment product. You will quickly end up with an intimate knowledge of whatever type of property you have chosen to specialize in and, when potential sellers interview you and one or two other agents about listing their investment property, you will shine like a new penny and stand a much better chance of getting the listing.

Because you will only be prospecting and talking to owners of this particular type of property, you will be in contact with them more often, you will have better, more interesting conversations with them, and they will come to know and respect you much sooner than if you are "shotgunning around" all over the place.

This doesn't mean that you can't sell other investment property; it just means that you will limit your prospecting and listing activities to a particular type of commercial investment.

Back in the 1970s, when I owned my own real estate firm, I specialized in Victorian apartment house sales in San Francisco. I kept learning until I had an intense knowledge of apartment house sales *and* knew almost all of the special features found in Victorian buildings.

I had about 350 owners in my database, and I mailed an informational letter with a return postcard every month. After several months, as they began to know and trust me, they started sending the postcards back to me requesting more information about buying more units, selling their apartment building, or exchanging their building for a bigger one or one in a better location. If I had not decided to specialize as I did, I would have never built the types of trusting relationships that I did. It made me a lot of money!

When I went to work for a major commercial investment real estate firm in Phoenix in 1999, I was asked to specialize in retail shopping centers. It only took about five months before I had developed relationships where people were seriously talking about listing their retail centers with me or buying another one through me.

Even though I had been a broker for over twenty-seven years, I still had to go through their training program in California. When I started with them, the first thing that they did was to give me a digital camera and tell me to take a picture of every retail shopping center in the greater Phoenix metro area and build a comparable sales book. There were hundreds of retail centers! But can you guess what happened? I really started to know which retail centers were where, what they had sold for, who the owners were, who the tenants were, what vacancies were where, how to spot a center that was thriving versus one that was struggling, and which ones were well managed or poorly managed.

Can you imagine trying to gain all of this knowledge for every type of commercial investment type? It would be impossible. That's why, when I would cold-call a retail center owner somewhere in the United States and he *That's the kind of credibility that gets people to respect you and do business with you.* would ask me questions about retail centers in the Phoenix metro area or even about his property, I had good, solid answers. That's the kind of credibility that gets people to respect you and do business with you.

I mentioned earlier about building a comparable sales book for the type of property or properties that you are specializing in. I found that the best format was to get a thick three-ring binder. Put a bunch of plastic inserts into it so you can put each comparable sale, or "comp," into the plastic and can move them around easier.

Put tabs in the binder with each city typed on them. Then, as you make up each comp sheet, you can just insert it in the proper city in ascending order by sold price. They are very easy to move around that way as you keep adding to your binder.

When I was taking the pictures, I would take them in jpeg format, which numbers them automatically. Then I had a spiral notebook that I had numbered from 1 to 350. As I took each picture, I would put the address down, if it was available, or the name of the center and the location (e.g., Safeway Center @ NE corner of Scottsdale Blvd & Shea). That way you don't get the pictures and centers mixed up.

This "comp" book is a mainstay of credibility for you, especially when you meet face-to-face with an owner to talk about listing his or her property. You have one or more pictures of each property, the sales price, the cost per square foot, the location, the name of the retail center or apartment complex, and the date of the sale. It is very impressive and will help you to quickly gain credibility and get more commercial listings and sales. *This "comp" book is a mainstay of credibility for you, especially when you meet face-to-face with an owner to talk about listing his or her property.*

5

Client Acquisition Techniques

Prospecting

*P*rospecting has to reign supreme when it comes to creating a data-base of commercial property owners that will do business with you. Several forms of prospecting are effective.

Cold calling is an excellent form of prospecting. I know, I know, you *hate* cold calling! When it came time to cold-call residential home-owners, so did I, and it took a lot of discipline to do it regularly back in the 1970s. (I haven't done any since then.) If you have read my second book, *How to Become a Mega-Producer Real Estate Agent in Five Years,* then you read the four interviews that I did with Mega-Producer agents who consistently sell from $40,000,000 to over $120,000,000 worth of real estate each year. None of them has ever cold called!

Now you're thinking, "Well, if they don't do it, why should I?"

The answer lies in what your competi-tion in the commercial arena is doing, and they are doing plenty of cold call-ing! You see, cold-calling commercial property owners is, for the most part, very different from cold-calling home-owners. You have very little to offer a homeowner when you call, after check-ing the national Do Not Call list. With all of the information available on the Internet, many if not most homeowners have at least a general idea what their home is worth. What else can you share with them except for neighborhood activities and such?

You see, cold-calling commercial property owners is, for the most part, very different from cold-calling homeowners.

Commercial property owners are very different. You have much to share with them. A large percentage of them do not even live in the same state as the property that you are calling them about. They are almost always very receptive to getting up-to-date information about what is going on in the commercial arena that will affect their investment holdings. Commercial business owners are also exempt from the Do Not Call list.

Commercial business owners are also exempt from the Do Not Call list.

If you really want to make your cold-calling experiences the most profitable that they can be, take the time to write each investor an introductory letter first. Tell the investors that you specialize in whatever their commercial holdings are and that as a way to get to know them, you will be sending them a complimentary newsletter on a regular basis. Tell them that you would like to hear about what topics regarding commercial real estate would interest them the most and that you will call them in a few days to quickly touch bases and see what interests them.

Look for real estate articles in the local papers, on the Internet, and in any trade magazines that you subscribe to. Compile them each month and write your own letter, citing the articles by reference, mailing them a copy of one or more articles, or reprinting them with permission. If you are a REALTOR®, then you get *REALTOR®* magazine each month; it has a commercial section in it with some very good articles.

Your first call should be to introduce yourself, to see if they got your letter and whatever article you sent along with it, to learn how they feel about the property they own now, and to ask if you may continue to send them local and national information about commercial real estate and especially information about the type of commercial property they own now or would like to own.

With their approval, you should start sending them something regularly and then follow up to see that they got what you sent and what their opinion of it is, or what else would they like to know. It is much easier than you think!

Make a regular work habit of driving by all of the investment properties that you have in your database every couple of months. Note if you see a vacancy sign or a building getting rundown or in need of a roof or some other obvious repair. When you talk to the owners, tell them about what you have seen. Offer to take a digital picture and e-mail it to them.

Make a regular work habit of driving by all of the investment properties that you have in your database every couple of months.

If another property in close proximity to theirs comes up for sale, get the information about it and send it to the person, or people in your database who have similar properties or who have told you that they are looking for a property similar to that.

Call and ask if they got the information and would they have any interest in acquiring the property through a purchase or an exchange of their existing investment.

Once you have amassed a database of properties of various sizes and locations, if an investor tells you that he or she is looking for a new investment of a certain size, a certain location, or a certain return on investment, all you have to do is go through your database to see if anyone there has a property that reasonably matches what is wanted. If they do, then call them and tell them that you have a client looking for an investment that their property seems to be a reasonable match for, and ask whether they would consider selling their property or exchanging it for something else as you may have a buyer for it. This can create a significant amount of business.

Have I made my case for how easy it is to cold-call commercial property owners yet? I hope so, because if you don't do it, you are in for a disappointing tenure as a commercial agent.

Referrals

Referrals from other agents is another form of prospecting that is very effective. Most residential agents do not have the knowledge to handle commercial investment sales. They are often not even allowed to handle them because of their company's policies and procedures. If they are a REALTOR® who must subscribe to the Code of Ethics, then they must give written notice to a potential client that they are unskilled in that type of property sales, if that is factual.

Getting a list of the top one hundred to two hundred residential agents in your market is easy to do and also can reap you big rewards in referrals of commercial listings and investors if you are consistent in your contact with these people. Be sure to keep good notes about who does and does not refer to you, and be sure to reciprocate with residential leads as often as you can.

Getting a list of the top one hundred to two hundred residential agents in your market is easy to do and also can reap you big rewards in referrals of commercial listings and investors.

Getting a relationship started with these agents is very similar to what you would do with your investor database, except that you will do an initial letter that explains what you have in mind, which is a mutual referral agreement where you will help each other build your businesses to new heights by referring business to each other. After that, you can keep in touch by a tasteful postcard or even e-mail. I highly recommend that each time you get a referral from someone, you immediately send them a handwritten thank-you note.

If you have built up a fairly strong residential following and are now at a company where you cannot service the needs of those people any longer, then you are a prime candidate to reap big rewards from this type of referral relationship. Just be sure to make it very clear that you will expect referrals in return in order to continue the relationship. Be sure to pick your referral sources carefully as you will want your loyal residential customers to be happy with whomever you refer them to. It should be clearly understood by your referral recipients that all commercial transactions with your referral clients will continue to be done through you only.

6

Property Valuation Methods and Tax Consequences

*I*ncome properties are evaluated by real estate professionals and appraised by appraisers according to the amount of gross or net operating income they produce as well as other factors such as location, condition, amenities, and the strength or weakness of the real estate investment marketplace at the time of the appraisal. These factors can vary greatly, and one particular method of valuation is most often more accurate than another, depending on the type and size of the investment property you are analyzing.

There is one constant in analyzing any property's value that you must strictly adhere to as a real estate professional: you must conduct a thorough rental survey of similar properties prior to your analysis so that you have current rent levels as of the date of your analysis. This will allow you to see if the property you are evaluating has rental rates that are at market or under market. Anything short of that is an incomplete analysis and may subject your client to a huge monetary loss and you to potential litigation, so make it one of your professional standards to always conduct a rental survey prior to any analysis.

Make it one of your professional standards to always conduct a rental survey prior to any analysis.

In addition, if you are involved in commercial real estate, you should seriously consider subscribing to CoStar and/or Loop-Net. These are commercial real estate databases that an agent can access for a monthly fee; they contain a significant amount of data about all types of commercial properties in any given metropolitan area, including property types; site addresses; owners' names or the name of a contact person; whether owned by a limited liability corporation (LLC), corporation, trust, or other entity; comparable sales data; and much more.

The methods of valuation are gross rent multiplier (GRM) method, capitalization of net operating income method (cap rate), market-data method, and internal rate of return (IRR) method. Now that we know what they are, let's look at each one and see when they are commonly used.

Gross Rent Multiplier Method

The gross rent multiplier or GRM method is most commonly used with small residential income properties, usually with around two to fifteen or twenty units. This method, although widely used, is often the least accurate of all of the valuation methods. The reason is that it simply looks at other recent local sales, takes their selling price, and divides it by the stated gross rents to arrive at a "times gross" factor. That factor is then multiplied by the subject property's gross rents to determine the value. It does not take location, amenities, condition (the existence or absence of deferred maintenance), lot size, date of sale, current rent levels, or vacancies into account. Because any one of these issues can affect the subject property's value, to ignore them is to inaccurately assess the subject property's value in many if not most cases. This method is still widely used in valuing small apartment buildings as cap rates are very often all over the board. However, be sure to take the other factors into consideration before making a value judgment.

Example: You are analyzing the value of a ten-unit apartment building. Its scheduled rents are $500 per unit per month, or $60,000 per year. Other buildings in the area have been selling for nine times their gross annual rent, so you value this building at $540,000 (9 × $60,000 = $540,000). It sounds good, but what if the market rents, based on your newly conducted rental survey, show that the units could be rented at $600 per unit per month? Using the same GRM, the building is now worth $720,000 ($600 × 10 = $6,000/month or $72,000/year gross rents), and you would have undersold it for your client by $180,000. Is this a malpractice issue?

Another example would be if you were analyzing two identical buildings that were side by side. One building, which was in good shape and completely rented, sold for ten times gross income a month ago. The building next door is poorly managed and has a 20 percent vacancy rate. Are they worth the same amount of money? Of course not, and strict adherence to the GRM method without considering all issues would give you an incorrect valuation of the property.

Any time that you use the gross rent multiplier as an indicator of value, you *must* look all of the issues described here to see if adjustments need to be made that will affect the value of the property.

Capitalization of Net Income Method (Cap Rate)

We can't talk about cap rates without revisiting something we learned in real estate school when we first became licensed. Do you remember IRV?

IRV is an acronym, usually placed in a triangle (see the example):

I = income (net operating income)

R = rate of return (as expressed as a percentage)

V = value

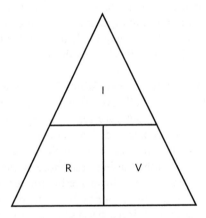

To find a property's income, you multiply the value by the desired rate of return.

Example: Income = $1,000,000 × 8% (0.08) or $80,000.
(This is NOI.)

To find a property's rate of return (cap rate), you divide the income by the value.

Example: Rate of return = $80,000/$1,000,000 or 0.08 (8%).

To find a property's value, you divide the property's income by the desired rate of return.

Example: Value = $80,000/8% (0.08) or $1,000,000

This method gives you a more accurate snapshot of the property's value as of a given day or date in time and essentially tells you what your return on your investment would be if you had paid cash for the property. It should still be preceded by a current rental survey, but it is arrived at by taking the gross scheduled income (GSI)—rents and other income such as parking and laundry, and deducting for vacancy and bad debt allowances to arrive at the gross operating income (GOI), then deducting the operating expenses to arrive at net operating income (NOI).

The next step is to assess the risks taken by owning the property and determine what return on your investment you would require, taking the risk of owning the property into consideration. If other buildings in the area have been selling at a capitalization rate of 8% (net operating income divided by sales price = 8%), then, if your rental survey shows that this building could achieve or is achieving a net operating income of $80,000, you would divide $100,000 by 8 percent ($100,000/0.08 = $1,000,000 value), as shown.

Is this method completely accurate? While it is usually much more accurate than the GRM, you still have some work to do. What if the current NOI is only $80,000, but your rental survey finds good demand in the area, and your client could increase the net rental income to $100,000 within six months? Should he or she pay $1,250,000 for the property and still take on the burdensome chore of increasing the rents and the vacancies that may arise by increasing the rents? Probably not; instead, you would value the property somewhere below the maximum value that *could* be achieved because of the risk assumed by the new owner and the loss of *scheduled* rents that he or she would realize until they did increase the rents.

You would use an annual property operating data (APOD) sheet to do an analysis of this type. The APOD also allows for the deduction of *debt service* (loan payments) to arrive at pretax cash flow. One has been supplied for you in the appendix of this book. The APOD details the following information:

- *The top portion* allows for placement of the date the form is filled out; the property's list price or any other price being analyzed; existing and new or proposed financing; the purpose of the APOD (for analysis purposes, put "Broker's

Reconstructed Statement"); the name of the property, if any; the address or location of the property; and assessed or appraised values.

- *Gross scheduled rental income* is the amount of rent that could be obtained if the property were 100 percent full all the time.

- *Other income* is for coin-operated laundry income, garage rentals, and any other income-deriving activities on the premises.

- *Vacancy and credit losses* allow for the real world where vacancies occur and people skip out on rent.

- *Gross operating income* is the real-world income the property is currently bringing in or the amount it would bring in on a pro forma basis per your rental survey.

- *Operating expenses* detail the actual costs to operate the property. Be very careful to see that these are accurate and reasonable. This sometimes entails calling utility companies, property management companies, and other product or service suppliers to get or verify information about the actual cost of a particular item or service. Try to estimate the new property taxes when filling out an APOD as it will give a more accurate net income figure to your client.

- *Net operating income* is the amount left over after all income is collected and all operating expenses are paid. This is the figure used to calculate a capitalization rate and is the amount left over to pay for any debt servicing (loans) on the property.

- *Debt service* is the amount of money necessary to pay any loans and is deducted from the NOI.

- *Cash flow before taxes* is any remaining money after all operating expenses and debt servicing is paid. This is the figure that is used to calculate the "cash-on-cash" return for the property being analyzed.

Cash-on-Cash Method

The cash-on-cash value of a property is determined by dividing the pretax cash flow by the down payment or total equity in the property. If a property is financed, or will be, the interest rate of the existing or new financing will have an effect on the cash-on-cash return of the property. The higher the interest rate, the lower the return because more of the net operating income is used for debt servicing.

Market Data Method

The market data method is always used in evaluating owner-occupied, single-family homes and condominiums. It is often used to evaluate rental property if there have been several similar types of property sales in the immediate area, and it is always used in conjunction with the "cap rate" approach if the property being analyzed produces an income stream. It is always used to evaluate land and other types of non-income-producing real estate such as a church or school. When analyzing the value of non-income-producing improved property, the market data method is used in conjunction with the depreciated replacement cost method.

Using this method, you arrive at the value of a property by comparing it with other similar types of property that have sold recently, usually within the past six months, if possible, and as close in proximity to the subject property as possible.

Although a rental survey is not conducted if there is no income being produced, the evaluation process still requires making comparisons of the comparable sales—or "comps," as they are called—then making adjustments to value based on such factors as date of sale; utility and zoning; availability of utilities, as in the case of land; condition and size of the structure(s) included in the sale, and their overall condition; and the strength or weakness of the market.

A good example of why this is important is a land sale that was being negotiated by one of my commercial guys as this book was being written. He wrote an offer on 126 acres of land in southern Arizona for $2,100,000. During the feasibility study period, he found that nearly thirty acres either was in a flood zone and not buildable or abuts an Indian reservation and has restricted use. Needless to say, the price was renegotiated.

Commercial properties requiring the use of the market data method of analysis and/or the depreciated replacement cost method are often undertaken by a certified appraiser with a Member of the Appraiser's

Institute (MAI) designation, or equivalent, and often cost several thousand dollars.

Internal Rate of Return Method

The internal rate of return (IRR) method of valuation is most commonly used by institutional investors such as real estate investment trusts (REITs), corporations, and other entities that often have multimillion- to multibillion-dollar investments in real estate holdings. They often tend to hold their properties for longer periods of time, and the IRR method gives them a better assessment of what type of return they may expect from a given property over a period of years.

The IRR method is usually calculated for at least a five-year period and calculates several things: the pretax cash flow of a property; the after-tax cash flow of a property, taking depreciation into account; and the overall return on the investment, including the reinvestment of the after-tax cash flows into optimum interest-bearing accounts.

The internal rate of return method is usually calculated for at least a five-year period and calculates several things.

If you take the courses offered by the REALTORS® national Marketing Institute that qualify you for the CCIM designation, you will learn how to do an IRR calculation and receive all of the necessary forms to calculate one. Several computer programs are available that will do it for you.

In our discussion of the internal rate of return method of evaluation, we touched on the pre- and after-tax consequences of real estate ownership. Let's take a few minutes here to talk about what you should know about real estate taxation and tax shelter issues.

Prior to 1986, investors were enjoying what was called the accelerated cost recovery system (ACRS) of depreciation allowance on their income taxes, which meant that anyone could buy an income property and depreciate it, or write the cost of the improvements off on their income taxes over a fifteen-year period. In 1986, this all came to a screeching halt. David Stockman, treasury secretary in the Reagan administration, was responsible for what is referred to as the Tax Reform Act of 1986, and it has changed the landscape of investment real estate ownership ever since.

New rules have been put into place that, as a real estate professional, you need to be aware of. A limitation has been placed on who qualifies to take a depreciation allowance on their income tax return. The new rules state that taxpayers with an adjusted gross income of less than $100,000 can use real estate losses (which are considered passive losses) to shelter up to $25,000 of their active income. Taxpayers whose adjusted gross income is between $100,000 and $150,000 lose $1 of this $25,000 maximum for each $2 that their adjusted gross income exceeds $100,000.

New rules have been put into place that, as a real estate professional, you need to be aware of.

If investors do not actively manage their property (active management includes hiring a property manager), then they are precluded from sheltering active income. Because investors have no management responsibilities in investments such as limited partnerships and REITs, the investor cannot use such passive or "paper" losses to shelter active income.

You, as a real estate professional, can use passive losses from investment property to offset other income without any limitations if you meet specific criteria, which include devoting at least 750 hours during the tax year to property management activities.

In a recent U.S. Supreme Court ruling, *D'Avanzo v. United States of America,* the Court ruled that Andrew M. D'Avanzo, who was not a real estate licensee, could not take advantage of unlimited depreciation allowances and was subject to the $25,000 limitation. D'Avanzo claimed that he managed his properties full-time and was therefore a real estate professional even though he was not licensed as a real estate agent, and he should be eligible for the unlimited treatment that licensees enjoy. The Court disagreed, holding that this allowance is limited to real estate professionals who meet the 750-hour annual test.

The improvements of residential real estate are currently written off over a 27.5-year period while nonresidential property is written off over a 39-year period. **Remember: you *must* deduct the land prior to making a depreciation calculation!**

Remember: you must deduct the land prior to making a depreciation calculation!

Example: You are a qualified investor and you own a twenty-unit apartment house that you paid $2,000,000 for, including your non-recurring closing costs that also attach to your property's adjusted cost basis. The county assessor has the allocation of land to improvements on your tax bill at 25 percent land and 75 percent improvements, so you use the same ratio.

To calculate the annual straight-line depreciation allowance that you could take as a deduction on your income tax return, you would take the following steps:

1. Compute the original cost basis (purchase price + nonrecurring closing costs).

2. Determine the allocation of land and improvements.

3. Deduct the value of the land.

4. Determine whether the property is residential or nonresidential. Use twenty-seven and a half years for residential and thirty-nine years for nonresidential.

5. Using the federal tax table shown here, find the month the property was put into service by the taxpayer. In this example, the property was put into service in September, so you would go to column 9 and the first year (row 1) to find the percentage figure of 1.061 percent (0.0161).

6. Compute the depreciation by multiplying the depreciable basis by the appropriate percentage found in the chart.

Federal Tax Table for Depreciation of Real Property (%).

General Depreciation System Method: Straight line **Recovery Period:** 27.5 years

The month in the first recovery year the property is placed in service:

Year	1	2	3	4	5	6	7	8	9	10	11	12
1	3.485	3.182	2.879	2.576	2.273	1.970	1.667	1.364	1.061	0.758	0.455	0.152
2–8	3.636	3.636	3.636	3.636	3.636	3.636	3.636	3.636	3.636	3.636	3.636	3.636

General Depreciation System Method: Straight line **Recovery Period:** 39 years

The month in the first recovery year the property is placed into service:

	1	2	3	4	5	6	7	8	9	10	11	12
1	2.461	2.247	2.033	1.819	1.605	1.391	1.177	0.963	0.749	0.535	0.321	0.107
2–39	2.564	2.564	2.564	2.564	2.564	2.564	2.564	2.564	2.564	2.564	2.564	2.564

$2,000,000 property value (including nonrecurring closing costs) — $500,000 land value (25 percent per assessor)

= $1,500,000 total depreciation allowed

Use 27.5 years since the property is residential.

Because our example puts the property into service in September, go to line 1, column 9 of the 27.5 chart. You see the taxpayer could take 1.061 percent, or $15,915, of the cost of the improvements off his or her tax return in the first year of purchase. Each year thereafter a deduction of 3.636 percent, or $54,540, could be deducted, subject to the $25,000 limitation.

Each time that you take a depreciation deduction on your income tax, you lower the "adjusted basis" of your property. If you subsequently sell your property, you will realize "gain" in two ways.

You will realize a capital gain (you hope!) by way of the property's increase in value that will be taxed at the rate of 15 percent of the net gain (if you owned it more than one year), and you will realize depreciation recapture that will be taxed at the rate of 25 percent. Depreciation recapture is the total amount of depreciation taken since you bought or exchanged into the current property. If you exchanged into it, then there may be additional depreciation recapture from prior property owned and exchanged into this one. *Always consult a tax professional prior to selling an investment property to assess the tax consequences!*

If you are representing a client in the sale or exchange of one or more investment properties, then you should always incorporate the following language into each purchase contract your client signs, for both the sale of the existing property and the purchase of the new one: "This sale is contingent on the written approval of the [here you would insert the word *purchaser's* or *seller's*] tax and/or legal counsel within 10 days after final acceptance of this agreement."

Tax-Deferred Exchanges

The tax laws change constantly as our legislators tend to use them to effect social change, but at this writing they are very favorable to real estate. As stated previously, if a taxpayer has owned a property for more than one year, he or she can sell it and only pay a 15 percent capital gain tax. However, if your client has already taken a depreciation allowance on it, then he or she will also pay a "depreciation recapture" tax on the amount of depreciation taken. This tax is currently at a 25 percent tax rate, so if your client is going to reinvest in other investment real estate he or she should consider doing a tax-deferred exchange for their new property acquisition to avoid paying a capital gain tax.

It is no longer necessary for the properties involved in a tax-deferred exchange to close escrow simultaneously. Under the current tax ruling, a taxpayer may do a "Starker" delayed exchange if they so choose. (See the bulleted example for a detailed explanation.)

While "simultaneous closings" and "direct deeding" used to be allowed, the Internal Revenue Service (IRS) has in recent years obtained a revenue ruling that states that an "intermediary" must be used for a tax-deferred exchange, or the IRS will disallow it. An intermediary is a qualified third party that acts as an escrow holder for the taxpayer's property or cash so that the taxpayer does not receive "constructive receipt" of either and have his or her exchange disallowed.

It works like this:

- Your client sells property A, subject to a tax-deferred exchange. An escrow is opened and an intermediary is named. Your client begins looking for a replacement property.

- Escrow closes and your client deeds property A to the intermediary, who then deeds it to the buyer. The cash proceeds from the sale of property A are given to the intermediary by the escrow company at escrow closing and are held on behalf of your client until a replacement property (B) is found. Easy enough, but there is a timing issue to deal with. Your client must "name," in writing, the property or properties he or she is going to acquire. No more than three properties may be named, and the aggregate total of the value of the named properties may not exceed three times the value of property A, or the exchange may be disallowed. Your client has forty-five days after close of escrow of property A to name the new property (property B) and the earlier of 180 days after close of Property A escrow or until the end of the next tax reporting period to close the exchange escrow, or the exchange may be disallowed.

- Your client finds a replacement property he or she likes. You make an offer on it for the client and get it accepted, subject to a tax-deferred exchange.

- The exchange escrow is opened, and your client assigns his or her rights in that purchase contract to the intermediary. The intermediary turns over your client's sale proceeds from property A to the escrow company.

- The exchange escrow closes and property B is deeded to the intermediary, who immediately deeds the property to your client through the exchange escrow.

If your client goes equal or up in value and loans, then he or she does not receive any "boot," and the exchange is totally tax deferred. If your client receives cash, personal property, or mortgage relief through the exchange escrow, whatever is received is taxable.

It is beyond the scope of this book to teach you all about tax-deferred exchanges, but if you are going to be working in the commercial real estate arena, then they will be an ever-present part of your life, and you should take classes that teach you more about them. The Women's Counsel of REALTORS® (WCR) and most of the title companies sponsor classes on tax-deferred exchanges from time to time, so contact your favorite title representative, real estate association, or the local WCR chapter for more information.

Internal Revenue Code section 1031, which deals with tax-deferred exchanges, is actually very small. It is the subsequent tax court decisions that give such weight and meaning to what may or may not be done. The more that you know about them, the higher the degree of professional service and advice you can give. I would especially advise you to learn about the *Biggs* decision and the *Mercantile Trust* decision that were handed down by the tax court.

7

The Annual Business Plan

January

1. Find where and when the next class on Section 1031 tax-deferred exchanges is, and sign up to attend.

2. Reread Part 2 of this book, and decide which type or types of commercial real estate you want to specialize in.

   Reread Part 2 of this book, and decide which type or types of commercial real estate you want to specialize in.

3. Have your favorite title company get you a detailed printout of every one of the commercial properties that you are going to specialize in and give it to you in such a fashion that you can place it in an electronic database.

4. With your list in hand, plan to spend at least two hours a day driving by and taking a digital picture of every property in your database. Stop at each property to get as much information about it as you can (i.e., retail tenants of a retail center, number of units of an apartment complex, etc.).

5. Research the owners or contact person of each property through the county assessor's records, CoStar, or Loop-Net.

6. Write an introductory letter to send to each contact person that tells them who you are, who your company is, what you are attempting to do (expand your client base by meeting and providing a service for them so that they will come to know you and, hopefully, use your services when they need investment real estate help now or at a later date).

7. Call each contact person two or three days after you have sent them your introductory letter. Tell them you are calling to see if

they got your letter and will allow you to include them in your database so that you can send them regular information about commercial real estate in the local community and a quarterly rental survey.

Note: After each phone contact that you make, no matter what the outcome is, send the contact person a handwritten thank-you note for the time that they spent with you. This is critical!

8. Make a decision about how you are going to approach your commercial real estate career (i.e., do residential while you transition or work for a commercial firm right away).

Note: If you join a large commercial firm, plan on prospecting at least five hours a day every day, six days a week. You will also spend about two hours a day researching contact people for each property and about two hours a day "driving the territory."

February

1. Continue to drive your marketing area and take pictures of properties.

2. Start to build a comparable sales book (comp book). This book will be broken down and tabbed by city; then each city will be broken down by sold price in either ascending or descending order. Use plastic holders for each comp so that they may be readily moved around as you get new comps. Each page should have a picture of the property and whatever data (e.g., address, sold price, cost/square foot, per unit cost, cost/acre, etc.) that you feel are important comparison points.

3. Start to prepare your listing proposal book. This book will be what you show potential sellers and will include information
   Start to prepare your listing proposal book.
   about your company and about you, including any letters of reference, your marketing plan, a reference to your comp book (which you will take with you on listing proposal meetings), and your estimate of the property's value and how you arrived at it.

4. Research contact people for each property.

5. Send introductory letters to contact people.

6. Make follow-up telephone calls to contact people to personally introduce yourself.

7. Research what investment groups, such as the local CCIM chapter, or other regular meetings of commercial brokers are available in your community, and plan to attend regularly. This gives you a forum to present your new commercial listings to other commercial real estate professionals, lets you in on new commercial listings that are available, and starts to give you credibility with the existing commercial broker network that exists in your city or metropolitan area.

8. Check with your local, state, and national associations' education departments to see what they have to offer in the way of educational materials that you can buy that will teach you more about commercial real estate. Buy at least three a year.

9. Refine your listing proposal book.

10. Drive by any new listings that you hear about, and call and get information on them.

Note: The informational package that the listing broker puts together is referred to as a "setup." Each time you get a setup on a property, be sure to update your database.

March

1. Continue to drive your market area and take pictures of the properties that you are specializing in, and gain as much knowledge about each one as you can.

2. Continue to build your comp book.

3. Send out any first-time letters to new contact people.

4. Call contact people to introduce yourself. Send thank-you notes.

5. Attend the CCIM chapter meeting. Get to know people, present your listings, and hear about new listings.

6. Refine your listing proposal book.

7. Drive by any new listings, and call and get a setup on them.

8. Get the names of two well-referred property management agents and leasing agents who specialize in your type of commercial property. Call them and offer to take them to lunch as a get-acquainted gesture. Ask them about current rental rates and vacancy rates in the area that you service.

9. Conduct a rental survey.

   Conduct a rental survey.

   Note: The results of your rental survey are very well received by the property owners and contact people you meet, and these results are an excellent reason to call them to see if they would like to receive a quarterly report from you.

10. Conduct listing proposal appointments, and show property as needed.

April

1. Drive the area and continue to add properties to your database.

2. Continue to build your comp book.

3. Research new contact people for properties entered into your database.

4. Send introductory letters to contact people.

5. Make follow-up phone calls to new contact people.

6. Make follow-up calls to any contact people that have expressed an interest in buying or selling.

7. Refine your listing proposal book.

8. Attend the local CCIM chapter meeting.

9. Drive by any new listings that you hear about; call and get a setup on them.

10. Conduct listing proposal appointments and show property as required.

11. Initiate and send out your quarterly newsletter with your rental survey results.

May

1. Drive your area and continue to take pictures of properties to add to your database. Stop and get any available "for lease" information on them as well.

2. Update your comp book.

3. Research the names of contact people, and send out your initial letters to them.

4. Make follow-up telephone calls to new contact people. Send thank-you notes.

5. Check in with existing clients to see what they need.

6. Attend a commercial real estate seminar. (CI 101 is a good example of an excellent class to attend as it will start you on the road to your CCIM designation.)

7. Attend the local CCIM chapter meeting.

8. Drive by any new listings you hear about; call and get a setup on them.

9. Conduct listing proposal appointments and show property as required.

June

1. Add properties to your database.

2. Update your comp book.

3. If you have finished completing your database, start to double-check it for accuracy. For retail properties, this will entail driving your territory all over again to check for vacancy signs and new retail tenants. For apartment complexes, this will mean verifying that the same resident manager is still there.

4. Drive by any new listings that you have heard about, and call and ask for a setup.

5. Drive by, take a picture, and gather information on new properties for your database.

6. Call your leasing or property management contact for lunch. Ask about current rental rates and vacancy factors.

7. Call your existing clients and see what help they need.

8. Conduct your quarterly rental survey.

9. Attend the local CCIM chapter meeting.

10. Conduct listing proposal appointments and show property as required.

July

1. Drive your territory and refine your database.

2. Update your comp book.

3. Contact all of your existing clients and see what help they need.

4. Contact any new property owners that you have entered into your database.

5. Update your database (recheck current contact person's or owner's name).

6. Attend the local CCIM chapter meeting.

7. Drive by any new listings, and call and get a setup.

8. Update your listing proposal book (new letters of reference, etc.).

9. Send out your quarterly newsletter with your latest rental survey results.

10. Conduct listing proposal appointments and show property as required.

August

1. Drive your territory. Look for new properties to add to your database. Look for new property management signs and new tenants if you are doing retail.

2. Update your comp book.

3. Call as many contact people in your database as you can. See if they are getting your newsletter, and ask if they need any help with any of their property. Send each one a thank-you note.

4. Attend a local seminar on investment property.

5. Attend the local CCIM chapter meeting.

6. Drive by any new listings that you hear about. Get a setup on them and update your database.

7. Call your existing and past clients and see if they need any help from you. Ask how they like your newsletter.

8. Conduct listing proposal appointments and show property as required.

9. Take a week-long vacation.

September

1. Drive the territory.

2. If you see any new construction of the type of property that you specialize in going on, get the names of the developers. Write to them; then call and see if you can have lunch or coffee with them. Let them know that you are an experienced commercial agent that specializes in their type of property. Ask if you could be considered the next time that they need brokerage services. Ask permission to put them on your mailing list, and tell them about your quarterly rental survey.

3. Update your comp book. Take any new pictures that you need to.

4. Call and have lunch with your property management or leasing agent contacts. Get any new vacancy rate or rental rate information from them that you can. Be prepared to update them on the state of the sales market as well.

5. Attend the local CCIM chapter luncheon. Present your listings.

6. Conduct listing proposal appointments and show property as required.

7. Send out introductory letters to any new contact people or new owners.

8. Call contact people and/or owners to keep in touch. Ask if they have any need for your services and if they are still getting your newsletter with the rental survey.

9. Drive by any new listings. Take a picture if you don't already have one. Call and get a setup, and change the information in your comps and your database.

10. Conduct your quarterly rental survey.

11. Conduct listing proposal meetings and show property as required.

October

1. Recheck your database to see that it is current. Make any changes that are necessary.

2. Send out introductory letters to any new owners.

3. Call your database contacts and introduce yourself to the new ones, and ask if they got your letter and if they would like to be put on your list and receive your quarterly newsletter with your rental survey. Send each one a handwritten thank-you note.

4. Send out your newsletter to your database, and call them a few days later to see if they got it. Ask if they need any help with their property. Send thank-you notes as appropriate.

5. Drive by any new listings that you have heard about. Get a setup and make changes in your database.

6. Update your listing proposal book as necessary.

7. Update your comp book.

8. Conduct listing proposal meetings and show property as required.

November

1. Drive your territory. Look at your properties, checking for any new construction or any new property management firms, leasing firms, or developers that you have found. Call each of them and introduce yourself as a commercial agent that specializes in their type of property and ask if you may be of any help. Ask if they would like to be put on your mailing list and receive your quarterly newsletter and your rental survey.

2. Update your comp book.

3. Update your listing proposal as required. Go in and indicate the properties where you have represented the buyer or seller.

4. Drive by any new listings. Get a setup and update your comp book and database.

5. Attend the local CCIM chapter meeting. Present your listings, and make note of any new ones presented by other brokers.

6. Conduct listing proposal meetings and show property as required.

December

1. Early in the month, send out "Happy Holiday" cards to as many people in your database as you feel is appropriate.

2. Call your property management or leasing agent contacts and arrange lunch. Get the latest news from them about vacancy rates and any changes in rental rates. Tell them about any new sale-related changes that you have become aware of.

3. Drive the territory and note any changes. Make introductory calls to any new property management firms, leasing firms, or developers. If you are doing retail, note any new tenants.

4. Attend the local CCIM chapter meeting if one is being held that month. Present your listings, get setups on new listings, and make the necessary changes in your comp book and your database.

5. Make as many calls as you can to your database, especially your existing clients, and ask if they need any year-end help with any of their properties.

6. Arrange a day to get away someplace quiet and create your next year's business plan. Each year should have more and more activities listed each month that are directed toward a particular person with whom you have been creating a relationship. Be sure to include vacations and time for those close to you.

7. Conduct listing proposal meetings and show property as required.

8. Do a year-end thorough assessment of your database. Delete anyone that you feel has become unproductive, and look for any changes that you missed throughout the year. Make special note of anyone that you feel will be productive for you this next year, and make a special notation to contact them in your appointment book at what you feel is an appropriate time next year.

9. Take a good look at your comp book to see that it is very up-to-date.

10. Assess your workload and see if it may be nearing time for you to hire either a part-time or a full-time licensed assistant.

8

The Listing Proposal

*T*his chapter describes two topics: the types of listing agreements that you may end up working with, and the listing proposal itself.

There are four types of listings that may be offered to you:

- Exclusive authorization and right to sell listing
- Exclusive agency listing
- Open listing
- Verbal listing

The only type of listing that offers you any reasonable assurance that you will get paid if the property sells is the *exclusive authorization and right to sell*. This type of listing is a mirror image of what is most commonly used in residential real estate. It states that you are the sole listing agent or agency and that you get paid no matter who represents the buyer in the purchase of the property. You will find resistance by many owners of commercial property to enter into this type of listing with you unless you and your firm are well known to them. This type of listing is used almost exclusively by the large commercial real estate firms.

> *The only type of listing that offers you any reasonable assurance that you will get paid if the property sells is the* **exclusive authorization and right to sell.**

The *exclusive agency listing* states that you are the exclusive listing agent and agency. However, the owner reserves the right to sell the property him- or herself to people whom you have not had negotiations with, and the owner owes you and your firm no commission if successful at selling the property him- or herself. It is easy to see the inherent problems with this type of listing. You and your firm could end up spending a lot of time and money marketing a property, only to have the seller find his or her own buyer. It is relatively easy for other real estate agents to go around you and make side deals with the owner so that they get a larger commission. In addition, if the owner is actively marketing the property, it can be very confusing for investors that see your ads and the owner's. The owner may even offer the same property at a lower price, and if your buyer happens across such an ad, it can hurt your credibility.

An *open listing* is in writing and sets the price and terms, but it states that it is cancelable "at will" and gives you no protection at all, except for tying down the price and terms. An open listing may be entered into with more than one broker at a time because it does not give any one broker the authority to act as the exclusive agent of the seller. Many sellers of commercial real estate will only offer this type of listing to an agent or agency that they do not know personally. Their main fear is that the property will be tied up for a period of time and that the agent or broker will not perform diligently. The drawback to you is that you could end up spending a lot of time and money finding a buyer only to have the seller decline your offer and look for others, or even go to your buyer directly and leave you out of the equation.

The last type of listing (or nonlisting) is the *verbal listing,* also known as a "pocket listing." In this instance, the property owner tells you verbally that you may work on the property and that he or she wants a certain price for it. The owner may also just tell you to bring offers and not even quote you a price. You do not want to get caught up in this type of quasi-marketing of someone's property. Even if the owner has quoted you a price, there is nothing binding about it. Let's say you represent the property to an investor as being available at a certain price. He likes the property and makes a really good offer that you take to the owner. The owner looks at your offer and says that she has changed her mind and doesn't want to sell any longer or that she may sell if you get your buyer to increase his offer considerably. You and the buyer that you are representing have very little, if any, bargaining power, and your credibility with your client has suffered greatly. You may even lose that person as a client.

If an owner wants to give you a verbal or open listing, what should you do? First, have a standard that you work by, and include in your standard that you will not work on anything but an exclusive authorization to sell. If someone offers you anything other than an exclusive authorization to sell listing, question why and address the owner's fears. As I stated earlier, the main reluctance to give you an exclusive is that you or your firm will not perform. When I was working in commercial real estate in the Bay Area, I got this type of resistance regularly. I overcame it by having a very detailed marketing and advertising plan with me when I met with the owners to discuss taking their listing. I would offer to make the marketing plan an addendum to the listing agreement. It stated that in the event that I did not perform each and every item in the agreement as stated, the owners only needed to give me notice of the breach; and if I did not cure the breach within twenty-four hours after their notification, they could cancel the listing. It didn't get me every listing, but it got me plenty!

If an owner wants to give you a verbal or open listing, what should you do?

Listing Proposal

Now let's discuss the listing proposal itself. What exactly is it, how long should it be for, and what does it contain that a residential listing agreement doesn't have?

We discussed earlier in this chapter the types of listings that are available. You will have to set your own standard as to the type of listing that you are willing to work with. If you go to work for a large commercial brokerage firm, then its standard will dictate, and you will almost certainly be working on exclusive authorizations only.

The firm that you work for will probably have its own version of a listing proposal or presentation. Many of these are really fine pieces of work, whereas some others need help. The large commercial firm that I worked for in Phoenix had a listing proposal that was a multipage PowerPoint product that could be altered as to comps and other details and be presented electronically or printed out and used in hard-copy format.

If your firm doesn't have a listing proposal for you, then you will need to create one. I suggest that you start with a white one-inch, three-ring binder that you can obtain at any office supply store. You will then need to break it down into sections.

Section 1 should have a few pages about the company that you work for. It should tell the sellers what the company is all about in as few pages as it takes to get the full message out. Too many pages in this section can become tedious for the seller and make them lose interest. As you start to go through this proposal with the sellers, keep in mind that everyone listens to their favorite radio station—that is, station WIIFM, or "What's In It For Me?" Each time that you present a page in your listing proposal, be prepared to present the benefit that is tied to it. People do not really care about features, except when they are tied to something that benefits them.

Section 2 should have your résumé and photocopies of any professional designations or college diplomas that you care to share with the sellers. Again, present your credentials as a feature tied to a benefit to the sellers.

Section 3 could be called *"What People Are Saying about Me"* and would contain any letters that you have received from satisfied customers. You should make a habit of asking for testimonials of this type after every transaction; they are worth their weight in gold! You can expect to have the sellers stop everything and actually read at least some of these, and it is interesting to watch the expression on their faces as they do. This is essentially a third-party sell of your credibility and skills.

Section 4 will have your marketing and advertising plan clearly stated. Be as detailed as you can, even to a weekly basis. It should clearly spell out where you are going to advertise and when, what type (by example) of brochure you are going to create, and who you are going to distribute them to and how often. It should tell the sellers how often you will see them personally as well as by telephone to update them on showings, interest from the public and from other brokers, and, in the event of no offers, it should call for a monthly meeting to discuss the pricing strategy.

Section 5 should have the appropriate comparable sales from your comp book (as an alternative, you can just take your comp book with you with the appropriate comps tabbed for easy access). You will also include the worksheet that shows how you arrived at your recommended asking and final sales prices, and a sheet that formally spells out your pricing strategy—that is, what you recommend as an asking price and the low and high recommended final sales prices.

Note: This listing proposal book, done properly, is a huge step in building the kind of trust in you the client will need in order to agree to give you an exclusive authorization listing, so take the time to make a really good one.

Now that we have created the listing proposal, let's talk a little bit about the actual presentation of your material to the potential sellers.

This listing proposal book, done properly, is a huge step in building the kind of trust in you the client will need in order to agree to give you an exclusive authorization listing.

Presentation

Everyone is different, and you will need to learn to size people up quickly in order to work with each one in a manner that that person finds agreeable. If you go into a meeting and spend a lot of time making small talk with a type A personality, this person will almost certainly not list with you and may just throw you out. You *will* have a lot of type A's in your database. When you interact with them, be "business polite" and to the point; they will really appreciate your directness. If, however, you are dealing with a person who is into relationships, then you will need to spend more time with "familiarization talk." These types really want to know about the person they are dealing with on a more personal level. There is no way to teach this skill; you will just learn it as you go along. If you err toward the latter type of interaction, with an eye or ear (if by phone) for signs of "Let's get to it," then you will soon develop great skill at reading people's preferences.

You very well may have already taken a picture of their property; if not, be sure that you do so as a part of your proposal. After the settling-in stage, compliment them on their property if it is appropriate to do so (I can remember a retail shopping center in Apache Junction, Arizona, that I was talking to a representative of an REIT about that had absolutely no redeemable qualities about it). If you don't know their plans regarding a tax-deferred exchange or sale, ask them what they propose to do with the sale proceeds and if you may be of any help in finding replacement property. Once you know their strategy, ask their permission to go through your proposal with them. It is a good idea to tell them about how long it will take and what it contains.

As you go through each section, keep an eye on the seller to see that he or she is still with you. Look for body language, voice inflection, and any other sign of boredom or sign that they aren't buying in to what you are putting forth. When you get to the comps, always make reference to "the market shows that . . ." in-

When you get to the comps, always make reference to "the market shows that . . ." instead of having it come from you.

stead of having it come from you. If the seller doesn't like the price that you recommend, you can make it the market's fault and not yours. Plan to spend a lot of time on how you arrived at the value you have placed on the property and on your marketing plan. These are the two areas that sellers will be the most focused on, and if they are presented correctly, you will have a good shot at getting the listing.

If, during the course of your presentation, you want to test the water to see if sellers are ready to list with you, you may want to state, "At some point I'll need a copy of your leases." Their reaction to open-ended questions or statements like this will often tell where they are at with regard to listing with you.

When you are through with your presentation, ask the sellers if there is anything that they would like for you to go over again or any other information that they need that you haven't supplied them with. This question shows a penchant for thoroughness on your part that sellers like to see, and it will often bring out any hidden objections that haven't been addressed yet.

A good final question is always "How do you feel about having [firm name] and me represent you?"

9

Writing the Purchase Contract

*I*f you are representing a commercial buyer in a small to midsize property acquisition, then you will probably use your company's or your local real estate association's commercial purchase agreement. The important thing to recognize here is that you do not want to use a residential purchase contract for the purchase of income-producing property. The reason is clear: you are helping your client purchase more than just bricks and stone—you are helping him to buy an income stream.

I don't know of a single residential purchase agreement that covers all of the issues that you need to address in the purchase of an income-producing property, and if you try to use that type of agreement, you will have to write in all of the commercial issues by hand. The chances of your omitting something important are just too great, so don't do it.

The commercial purchase agreements that are available today have evolved over many, many years and are all-encompassing now. You will need to have language in the agreement that makes the purchase contingent on several issues to protect your buyer, some of which are as follows:

- Inspection and approval of the interior of all rental units.

- Inspection and approval of all leases and/or rental agreements, including any garage leases and washer/dryer leases.

- You will need to see that the agreement is contingent on the inspection and approval of the accounting records showing all income and expense items for the past two years (at a minimum).

- There needs to be a provision for the buyer to receive estoppel certificates from all tenants prior to close of escrow. I have found that, all too often, real estate agents that hold themselves out as commercial specialists don't even know what an estoppel certificate is. It is a written statement signed by each tenant that states the tenant's name(s), the address and unit number of the premises that they occupy, the amount of rent that they are currently paying, the amount of any last month's rent and/or security deposit that the current owner or property management company is holding on their behalf, and a statement that they are not currently in bankruptcy proceedings or withholding rent from the owner for any reason (e.g., unsuitable living conditions, etc.).

Every one of these things is vitally important for your buyer to know about the property *before* he or she becomes the owner.

Every one of these things is vitally important for your buyer to know about the property before he or she becomes the owner.

As an example, I represented an investor in a tax-deferred exchange in San Francisco whereby he was trading into a ten-unit apartment house at the base of Nob Hill. The owner and the resident manager both told us what the current rents were, and we made our calculations as to the value from there. They were visibly upset when my offer required estoppel certificates—and no wonder. I became suspicious while we were looking at the interior of the units. I asked several of the tenants what their rent was, and I told them that they would be required to sign an affidavit to that effect. It then came out that they were paying the rent stated on the leases but were getting a cash "kickback" from the owner. He was trying to pump up the value of the building in this manner and would have been very happy to have my client inherit the whole mess. We made a requirement of getting new leases signed at the real rents and adjusted our offer accordingly. The tenants were actually relieved, the seller was so embarrassed that he went along with whatever we wanted, and the resident manager was fired.

Something that is not prewritten into most commercial purchase contracts is the written approval of the buyer's legal and/or tax counsel.

This is a must! You must see that every single commercial contract that you draft on behalf of a client says, "*This sale is contingent on the express written approval of the buyer's tax and/or legal counsel within ten days after final acceptance of this offer.*"

Sometimes your client will be totally satisfied with the transaction and won't go to an attorney or CPA. That's his or her choice; however, make sure that you give your client the right to do it as a contingency of the sale or exchange. Many attorneys don't like to give opinion letters, so I always include a "drop-dead" clause along with the previously cited contingency language that furthers that statement by saying, "*Any objections shall be made in writing within said ten days, or this contingency shall be considered waived by the buyer.*"

If your client is purchasing the property in the name of an LLC, trust, REIT, or other legally created entity, note right away that the title company will require a copy of the LLC agreement or whatever the entity is, to see that it will issue a title insurance policy on it. Some people will be reluctant to give it to you, but they must give it to the title company. Some clients like to make the offer in their name "and/or assignee." This gives them the contractual right to assign the purchase to literally anyone during the escrow period. Arizona law says that real estate purchase contracts are assignable unless there is a specific clause to the contrary in the purchase contract, but each state may be different, and you will need to be aware of the provisions in yours, as well as the provisions in the purchase contract.

Note: If you are the listing agent, and a contract is presented to you that says "and/or assignee," you may want to counter offer and make the buyer name any assignee within a short time instead of going the entire escrow period before you find out who the real purchaser is.

Be sure to give yourself sufficient time to conduct the escrow. The due diligence period is usually longer for income property than it is for a home purchase because there are more issues to investigate. The financing can also take longer to obtain as the lender may have many leases and the accounting records to review.

If your client has a property to sell to a third-party purchaser to effect a tax-deferred exchange, then you will most certainly want a longer escrow on the purchase "leg" of the transaction in order to allow sufficient time to market the property. You will also need to make the contract contingent on the sale of the buyer's property to a third-party purchaser within a certain number of days. That way, if you don't have the down-leg property sold in time to complete the exchange, you will not be in default on the contract and will not lose a deposit. You should insert the clause "*This sale/exchange is contingent on the sale of the buyer's property at [address] to a third-party purchaser within [number of days] after final acceptance of this offer.*"

Finally, it is clearly in your client's best interest, if he or she is doing a tax-deferred exchange, to have an "intent" clause in the contract. This should state, "*It is the sole intent of the buyer named herein to effect a tax-deferred exchange of the equity in the property commonly known as [address] for the equity in the property stated in line [number] of this contract. The seller agrees to cooperate with the buyer in said exchange, including the use of an intermediary, pursuant to IRC Section 1031 at no additional cost or liability to the seller.*"

> *It is clearly in your client's best interest, if he or she is doing a tax-deferred exchange, to have an "intent" clause in the contract.*

Note: **Please remember, the scope of this book is not to discuss how to practice law but to give you a good working knowledge of how to conduct yourself as a successful commercial agent. Please review all references to contract language with your own attorney and broker prior to use.**

When you are dealing in larger properties, where you often have a much more sophisticated buyer, it will be common for you to start the negotiations with a nonbinding letter of intent (LOI). A sample LOI is provided for you in the appendix, and its format can be easily duplicated on an Excel file.

This letter, which your client will sign, is a nonbinding letter that states all the major facts and issues under which your client will be willing to purchase a certain property. Once signed by your client, you will get it to the listing agent by fax or in some other fashion. Some type of verbal exchange will have taken place between you and the listing agent prior to your sending the LOI. However, when you finally do send it to the agent, be sure to include a short letter with your client's qualifications and any other pertinent information that will be important to the seller. This type of initial negotiation is very typical in the purchase of large tracts of land.

Once the major terms have been worked out in this manner, your client will almost always have his or her own attorney draft the actual purchase agreement. It will be a rarity for your client to have you draft the contract on your form. Your main function at this time is to communicate with the buyer's attorney to ensure that all of the terms and conditions previously agreed to are incorporated in the final draft of the purchase agreement. Your commission will often be included as a condition of this type of purchase agreement, but be sure that there is a written statement somewhere that clearly spells out the total agent compensation, who is liable to pay it, and when and how it is split. Failure to see to this matter will almost always make you the recipient of a "commissionectomy."

Failure to see to this matter will almost always make you the recipient of a "commissionectomy."

After you have drafted the purchase agreement and your buyers have signed it, give them a copy; then contact the listing agent, notify him or her of the offer, and ask how he or she would like to proceed. If possible, you should be there to present your buyers' offer in person; however, many owners do not live near their rental property, and the listing agent will need to fax the offer to them and discuss it with them over the telephone. If this is true, you should send a letter along with your contract that tells a little about the buyers and what qualifications they have that will make this a successful transaction. If you cannot be there in person to present the offer, be sure to send along any comparable sales you have that make your case regarding the offered price.

If you get a counteroffer that includes a price increase, complete another APOD at the new price before you meet with your buyers. This way they will be able to see what the counteroffer really means to them in terms of cash flow for the new property.

10

Conducting the Commercial Escrow

*T*here are, of course, two sides to every escrow: the seller's side and the buyer's side. Let's take each side and talk about the issues that must be addressed by the agent who is representing that side.

The Listing Agent or Seller's Representative

Once an agreement has been reached, escrow must be opened just as for a residential transaction. The purchase contract will usually dictate who opens the escrow and with whom; however, it is usually the buyer's agent who does it.

Your job as the seller's agent is to see that escrow is opened in a timely manner and that any deposit referenced in the purchase agreement has been placed into escrow by the buyer's agent. Because earnest money deposits must be placed into a neutral depository (escrow or broker's trust account) by the end of the following business day after an offer is accepted, if you haven't heard from the buyer's agent by late afternoon of the next business day, you need to call him or her and ask if escrow is opened. If not, probe as much as necessary to find out why. Is it a case of buyer's remorse or just a slow-moving agent?

Get the escrow company's name, escrow agent's name, phone and fax numbers, and the escrow number. In the eastern area of the United States, where closing attorneys are used, get the full information about the closing attorney. Call and verify that the deposit has been placed into escrow.

Create a time line for the escrow, and get a copy to all parties to the escrow, including the escrow company or closing attorney. This time line should outline

- the dates each contingency must be waived by,
- the dates any inspections must be ordered and/or conducted by, and
- the escrow closing date and any other dates stated in the purchase contract.

Creating and using an escrow time line is an excellent way to help conduct an orderly, efficient escrow.

As the seller's agent, you will need to get all leases and rental agreements, including parking agreements and washer/dryer rental agreements from the seller. Photocopy them and get them to the buyer's agent for the buyer's review. You will also need to help the seller get estoppel certificates signed by all of the existing tenants, and you will need to get the seller's Schedule C from his or her income tax statement for the number of years dictated by the purchase contract. Schedule C shows the income derived from the seller's building and the operating expenses. Nearly all commercial purchase contracts have a clause in them that makes the contract contingent on the buyer's review and approval of these items. Buyers often want at least the last two years of operating statements to review. Get what the contract dictates, make photocopies, and get the copies to the buyer's agent as quickly as you can.

Most commercial purchase agreements state that the sale is contingent on the buyer's written approval of the interior of all or a sampling of the rental units. In large apartment complexes, this can be a difficult chore to coordinate, and care must be taken to adhere to the tenants' rights by way of giving proper and timely written notice of your intent to enter their apartment. The same practice applies but is not as difficult with office buildings and is a little more difficult with medical buildings because of patient privacy issues.

As soon as the preliminary title report or abstract of title is available, read it over very carefully.

As soon as the preliminary title report or abstract of title is available, read it over very carefully. See that the names of the vested owners stated in the title report or abstract match the sellers' signatures on the purchase agreement, and carefully review the exceptions to title listed on Schedule B.

If the property is owned by a family trust, LLC, corporation, or other nonperson entity, get a copy of the trust agreement or corporate resolution, and give it to the escrow agent or closing attorney. The closing attorney or title company legal department will want to read the agreement prior to issuing a title insurance policy or giving an abstract of title.

If the property is financed, get all of the loan information from the sellers, including the lender's name, address, phone and fax information, and loan number, and give it to the escrow agent or closing attorney so that he or she can order any loan payoff demands when necessary.

Once these issues have been taken care of, your main job through the rest of the escrow is to keep the buyer and buyer's agent on track and to help your sellers negotiate repairs requested by the buyers and other such issues.

Whether you are representing the buyer, the seller, or, especially, both parties, it is a *must* that you keep a complete communication log in your file that lists every single item that you say and do during the entire escrow. Every phone call should be logged, including a brief statement of what was said. Each activity you do should be noted, along with the date and time. An excellent piece of advice is to get a handheld digital tape recorder, and when you do or say something having to do with an escrow, tape a message about it. About once a week, take out all of your escrow folders, and play back and transcribe the noted activities into your communications log.

> *An excellent piece of advice is to get a handheld digital tape recorder, and when you do or say something having to do with an escrow, tape a message about it.*

Why is this so important? If the escrow goes "sideways" and people start looking for someone to blame, they often get "selective memory" about things you told them, did for them, and so forth. In these instances, a good communication log is your very best friend.

Another point is to put everything in writing and convey it to whomever it must go to in such a fashion that you can prove you sent it or conveyed it. The best methods are as follows:

- If you e-mail something to someone, blind-copy (BCC) yourself, print out the e-mail, and put it in your escrow folder.

- If you fax something to someone, be sure to staple the fax cover sheet showing the date and time to what you faxed, put it in your escrow folder, and enter it into your communications log.

- If you hand-deliver something to someone, have an additional copy of whatever it is with you, and have the person sign "Received" and date it. Put it in your file and communication log.

The Selling Agent or Buyer's Representative

Most contracts dictate that the buyer selects the escrow agent, so the buyer's agent usually opens the escrow. If this is the case, you should open the escrow as soon as possible, but absolutely within the time prescribed by the contract or state law. Have all of your buyers' full names and their complete contact information with you when you open the escrow, and give it to the escrow agent or closing attorney along with the earnest money deposit. In most states, the purchase agreement also acts as escrow instructions; if this is true in your state, be sure to give the escrow agent or attorney a copy of the purchase agreement and any counteroffers and addenda as well. Ask the escrow agent to call the other broker and notify him or her of the escrow number and all necessary escrow company phone and fax numbers. Have the escrow agent verify to the listing agent that you have given the escrow agent the deposit check.

If your buyer is financing the purchase and you know who the lender is, ask the escrow agent to see that two copies of the preliminary title report are delivered to the proper loan officer at the lending institution as soon as he or she receives them. You should also get two copies. Read the report thoroughly! Check the owners' names referenced in the report against those given in the purchase agreement to see they match. Read Schedule B to see there are no exceptions to title that will adversely affect your client. Give a copy to your client, and get a written acknowledgment that he or she has received it. Usually a dated "Received" on another copy is sufficient.

Call the seller's agent and request copies of the leases, estoppel certificates, and accounting records specified in the purchase agreement (remember to log all of this into your communications log).

Set a mutually acceptable date and time to see the inside of the rental units if the contract calls for it. Call your buyer to verify the date and time with him or her.

Call the seller's agent and request copies of the leases, estoppel certificates, and accounting records specified in the purchase agreement (remember to log all of this into your communications log).

Get a copy of the purchase agreement to the loan officer, and ask if he or she has received the preliminary title report or abstract of title yet. Ask what income/expense documents he or she will need to process the loan, if applicable, and ask the seller's agent for them. Document this as well.

Once you have received the required income/expense documents from the seller, review them carefully, and make notes of anything that looks odd or suspicious; then call and clarify each item, if any, with the seller's agent. Make notes of all this. Take the documents to your buyer, and review them with him or her. Get copies to the lender if applicable.

During the due diligence period, you need to order any termite inspections or other reports that are mandated by the purchase contract, set a time to conduct them, and ask the seller's agent to notify the tenants if entry into any of their units is necessary. It is very wise to always suggest a termite/pest inspection and a roof inspection when representing a buyer in the purchase of any improved real estate as these can be "big ticket" repairs. If zoning or rezoning is an issue or a contingency of the sale, you need to get on it with the proper government authorities and/or legal representatives immediately as these things can take considerable time.

In certain areas, you need to check for flood zones, earthquake safety zones, city or county special assessments, and other matters. If you aren't very sure of yourself, ask a seasoned commercial agent in your area or your escrow agent what to watch out for. This is the period in an escrow when most issues of nonperformance by an agent occur that can lead to legal problems, so be extradiligent.

This is the period in an escrow when most issues of nonperformance by an agent occur that can lead to legal problems, so be extradiligent.

Once the due diligence period is over and everything is successfully negotiated or disclosed *in writing,* your buyer's new financing is approved, and all contingencies have been waived in writing, it is time to get the paperwork signed and close the escrow. You should always accompany your client (buyer or seller) to the escrow signing. Not only is it a professional standard that you should meet, but it also prevents a "commissionectomy" from taking place while you aren't there.

You should arrive at the closing at least fifteen to thirty minutes early and ask to review the closing papers. Have your calculator with you, and check the prorations, especially rents, security deposits, last month's rents, homeowners association (HOA) fees, if any, and real property taxes. If the escrow agent makes a mistake and debits your client when he or she should have had a credit, it is a "double hit" as your client not only didn't get the credit but got debited as well.

Call the seller's agent to make arrangements to pick up any keys and other items that are to be transferred to the buyer. Pick them up and deliver them to the buyer. It is a good idea to meet the buyer at his or her new property a day or two after closing just to check things out.

11

Marketing and Advertising Commercial Real Estate

*A*lthough similar in nature, marketing and advertising are actually somewhat different. Marketing is more about "branding" or making a name for a person or product, whereas advertising is more about getting a target audience interested in a specific product or service.

Advertising

Advertising commercial real estate is different than residential real estate. Commercial real estate investors don't go to open houses and seldom go into real estate offices looking for good investments to buy. They read the papers and go to the Internet, and many tend to rely heavily on their real estate broker.

If you are using the newspaper for your advertising, be sure to pick the correct paper. The local papers are not usually where investors spend much time; they opt for the larger regional newspapers that are more likely to have a greater number of investment properties listed in a separate commercial section. Because the investor will not be living in the investment, he or she will consider owning real estate farther away from where he or she lives, as long as it is managed properly.

> *Because the investor will not be living in the investment, he or she will consider owning real estate farther away from where he or she lives.*

Newspaper advertising is expensive, especially if you are using the *Wall Street Journal, USA Today,* or even one of the larger regional papers like the *San Francisco Examiner,* but such papers are also the most effective ones to use if you are selling a property that warrants that type of exposure. Because of the cost, you will want to keep your ad as small as possible while conveying enough information to make someone want to call you. People don't read newspaper ads—they scan them—so it is very important to follow the time-tested AIDA formula when you create an ad:

> **A**ttention—you need to get the reader to stop scanning and read your ad.

> **I**nterest—the first few words of your ad need to gain the reader's interest and make him or her want to read the rest of the ad.

> **D**esire—the rest of your ad needs to create a desire for more information and a desire to call you.

> **A**ction—the last part of your ad needs to urge the reader to take action, to call you for an appointment or for more information. Here's an example:

WELL-LOCATED GARDEN APARTMENTS

Excellent San Francisco suburb area with almost no vacancy.

80 garden units. Almost all 2-BR units. Long-term tenants.

6.5% cap rate,

$20,000,000 or your property in trade

Don't miss this excellent investment—call Bob Herd at 520-555-1010

This style of ad does several things:

- It tells the reader approximately where the property is without disclosing the exact location.
- It tells the reader the price.
- It tells the reader the return at the list price.

- It tells the reader the owner may take the reader's property in trade. (If the owner doesn't want the reader's property, you as the broker would list the reader's property if it isn't already listed, and you would seek a buyer for it to do a normal three-way exchange.)
- It tells the reader to act now by calling you for more information.

Be careful not to make your ad so small (to save money) that you turn it into an ineffective ad that won't get you any calls. Doing so is penny wise and pound foolish.

If you are new or newer at the commercial real estate business, call a few commercial brokers in your area and ask them where they get the best results from newspaper advertising.

Be careful not to make your ad so small (to save money) that you turn it into an ineffective ad that won't get you any calls. Doing so is penny wise and pound foolish.

The Internet

Every day more and more commercial brokers are using the Internet to advertise their listings. Your Internet site must achieve the same results as the newspapers in order for you to receive bona fide client inquiries. Your site must contain enough information to get an investor interested but omit just enough to make the investor call you.

If you would like to see an excellent site, I suggest you get on the Internet and go to eMarket at www.propertyline.com. A commercial broker named Mark Goldberg with MID-AMERICA Real Estate Corporation has several of his listings featured there, and they contain just enough information to get him calls from interested investors. It is a great format.

If you work for a commercial real estate firm, it may have a Web page on its Web site for you.

Marketing

As I said earlier, the lines are sometimes blurred between advertising and marketing. In addition to newspaper ads and the Internet, you should consider joining as many of the commercial real estate groups in your area as you can. Plan to attend their monthly marketing meetings as often as you can, even if you don't have a listing to sell.

These meetings regularly have educational sessions where you will learn things you just can't get elsewhere. They also have marketing sessions where commercial agents match up buyers with sellers and put transactions together. They are also a great place to get to know the other commercial agents in your area.

At this time there are almost no viable commercial multiple listing service (MLS) systems in the United States. The commercial agents just won't put their inventory in them because too many totally unqualified residential agents try to work on them, with horrible results. If you attend the local CCIM chapter meetings and other commercial meetings, you will get to know the "players"; once you gain their trust and respect, they will gladly share their inventory with you when you have a buyer.

If you attend the local CCIM chapter meetings and other commercial meetings, you will get to know the "players."

12

Financing

Single-family homes, condominiums, and owner-occupied apartment houses of four or fewer units are readily financed by savings and loans, savings banks, and mortgage brokers. However, these lenders do not ordinarily finance commercial real estate.

Apartment houses of five or more units and all other types of commercial real estate are usually financed by life insurance companies, commercial banks, mortgage bankers, and REITs.

The *mortgage underwriting* of an income-producing property involves much more analysis than is required for a home loan.

Risk Aversion

Although the real estate serves as the collateral for the financing, it is not the primary defense against loss to the lender. No lender wants to obtain ownership of a property through foreclosure due to a borrower's default. The lender's first line of defense against having to foreclose on a property is to reduce the probability of the borrower defaulting on the loan in the first place.

> *The lender's first line of defense against having to foreclose on a property is to reduce the probability of the borrower defaulting on the loan in the first place.*

The most effective means of ensuring prompt and continuous payment of a loan on income-producing property is to accurately forecast the income flow from which the debt servicing will be paid. This is a fundamental underwriting tenet.

Debt Coverage Ratio

Most lenders who finance investment real estate projects are concerned more with the relationship between net operating income (NOI) and annual debt service (ADS) than they are with the loan-to-value ratio. The reason for this is the general lack of agreement concerning the property's value and/or the overall rate used to capitalize the NOI.

The foundation of the value of income-producing real estate is the future income stream. The key to estimating the future value of this income rests in estimates of the *amount, timing, duration,* and *stability* of future income flows. The process of converting these future income flows to a present value is a simple matter of capitalization at the appropriate rate. In the area of mortgage lending on income-producing property, the appropriate rate can sometimes present quite a problem, particularly when the overall rate on the property combines such factors as the tax situation of the typical investor, typical financing terms, appreciation, and length of ownership of the investment.

As indicated earlier, the lender is not interested in acquiring the property by default. That is always the *final* step in protecting the money that has been loaned. The *first* line of protection is the *income stream,* for it is from the income stream that the lender will be repaid. Loan payments include interest on the loan and periodic principal payments. Thus, the lender is much more concerned with a careful examination and analysis of the validity of estimates of NOI than it is with estimates of the property's current market value.

Lenders use a *debt coverage ratio* to compare ADS with NOI. The debt coverage ratio is the NOI divided by ADS.

$$\text{Debt coverage ratio} = \frac{\text{NOI}}{\text{ADS}}$$

The lender's margin of safety—that debt payments can be met by the property's income—increases as the coverage ratio increases.

Example

A loan that requires ADS of $96,000, with an NOI of $120,000, would have a coverage ratio of

$$\frac{\$120,000}{\$96,000} = 1.25.$$

In this case, NOI could decline 20 percent (from $120,000 to $96,000) before the lender would have to rely on the owner to contribute to debt service from other financial resources.

Based on experience, lenders may specify a maximum debt coverage ratio for different types of property. In the case of an NOI that can be forecast with a high degree of accuracy with respect to size, duration, and timing, such as a long-term NNN lease with an AAA-rated tenant, the lender will usually require less margin between NOI and ADS, thereby giving a lower debt coverage ratio. Accordingly, an increased risk or uncertainty in the NOI will increase the DCR.

Based on experience, lenders may specify a maximum debt coverage ratio for different types of property.

Determination of Maximum Loan Amount

A lender will make a 7 percent loan with monthly payments for thirty years. The required debt coverage ratio for the subject property by that lender is 1.25. NOI is $96,000. First determine the monthly payment:

$$\frac{NOI}{Debt\ coverage\ ratio} = ADS$$

$$\frac{\$96,000}{1.25} = \$76,800$$

Monthly debt service (loan payments) are

$$\frac{ADS}{12} = \frac{\$76,800}{12} = \$6,400 \text{ per month.}$$

The maximum loan on the subject property is the present value of an annuity (the loan payments) at 7 percent per year with monthly compounding for 30 years. The known values are as follows:

Payment = $6,400 per period (month)

Amortization period = 30 (years) × 12 = 360 periods

Interest = 7%/12 = 0.58% per period

You would put the following values in your calculator:

$6,400 = PMT

360 = N

0.58 = I

$965,865 = PV (loan amount)

The maximum loan would probably be rounded to $966,000.

13

Conversations with Three Veteran Commercial Brokers

Note: Bob Herd's comments are in bold and italicized print; Paul Lindsey's, Kenneth Young's, and Mark Schneider's comments are in regular print.

Paul Lindsey, CCIM
Tucson, Arizona
Real Estate Brokerage

Paul, tell the readers a little about your background.

I began my real estate career in 1982 with a small full-service company. In those days, "full-service" meant everyone got to do everything because there was no such thing as specialization. I got my broker's license in three years and formed a commercial real estate investment company with several local businessmen as clients and struck out on my own.

After two years, I began to feel isolated from the people and information that are so important to the business, and I joined a growing commercial company as their number two leader. We grew the company to become the largest in our market, but by 1989, I became restless again.

Three of us from that company plus two other well-respected local commercial brokers formed Chapman/Lindsey Commercial Brokerage. I was the designated broker. We each specialized in certain product areas, with me as the main commercial investment broker. One of the other brokers focused on commercial property asset management, two others on land, and the third on retail leasing and brokerage.

In 1999, I was given the opportunity to bring Chapman Lindsey into a partnership with the local Coldwell Banker franchise as its commercial division. My partners balked at the move, but I saw it as a tremendous opportunity and left in the fall to become a 50 percent owner of the Coldwell Banker company, which was 99 percent residential—and still is. We grew that company from about $9,000,000 in gross commission income to about $40,000,000, greatly assisted by the strongest local real estate market in history.

In March 2005, the NRT, which is Cendant's real estate holding company, made us an offer that was based on a generous multiple of the prior twelve months' earnings, which was by far the strongest twelve months' earnings we ever had and was unlikely to repeat, so the decision to sell was fairly clear. We closed the sale in September 2005, and I stayed until the end of the year to assist in the transfer.

When you entered real estate, what made you decide to become a commercial broker instead of a residential broker?

My first broker encouraged me to do whatever interested me and supported me in exploring commercial brokerage and leasing. My prior life had been mostly business related, and most of my "sphere of influence" was the business community. I sold a few houses, but it became clear fairly early on that the challenge and complexity of the commercial brokerage world was where my passion rested. I was also lucky enough to have a wife with a steady salary!

You said you started with a small company and moved to a bigger one?

Yes, my first company had twelve agents, and three of them were owners. We all did whatever type of business came in the door. None of the others were really interested in commercial real estate, and I was not really interested in residential, so they began sending their commercial referrals to me. That was a nice way to start out, although most of them had little commercial experience to share with me, so most of my "training" was fairly informal.

That's interesting! What type of training did you receive?

I would take any commercial classes the local schools would offer, but there weren't many, and the quality was spotty. I started the CCIM program right away, although I had to wait several years to build the portfolio of transactions needed to earn the designation. I found the classes extremely interesting, and the people who attended were of a consistently high quality. By 1988, I had earned the CCIM designation. At that time there were only about three thousand in the whole industry and only about eight in Tucson.

You know, I took CI 101 through 104 and had the portfolio to get the designation, but I was running my own company then, and I didn't want to go to Chicago to take the last course. I really wish now that I would have!

Did you immediately start to specialize in one or two types of investment property types, or did you "do it all"? Did it change as you matured as a commercial agent?

I began focusing on the investment side of the market as opposed to the leasing or property management side. I was intrigued by the analysis that went into the decision-making process. Each area has its own vocabulary and eccentricities, so it is impossible to be an expert in all areas, but the basic analysis is the same whether it is an office building or an apartment complex. I enjoyed finding the best investment for my clients and helping them grow their portfolios.

What are your thoughts on specialization in one or two types of commercial real estate products instead of trying to do it all?

I always suggest agents make every effort to specialize, but sometimes that means trying many different things before you find the one that feels right or best to you. Possessing more information than the competition gives you a tremendous advantage that only comes with specialization.

I always suggest agents make every effort to specialize, but sometimes that means trying many different things before you find the one that feels right or best to you.

Q *What type of preparation did you do—such as build a "comp" book, drive the territory and learn where the various commercial properties were located, which properties had which types of tenants, and so on?*

Our market has always had a very cooperative commercial brokerage "fraternity," with agents very willing to share information. We never had a commercial MLS, so access to the commercial inventory has always been a challenge. Building strong relationships within the brokerage community is the best single step an agent can take. Keeping records in some organized way of the entire product in your geographic and specialty areas is critical, especially for leasing agents. Being able to access information about the size, ownership, tenant mix, and so on, of your market properties is basic but critical.

Keeping records in some organized way of the entire product in your geographic and specialty areas is critical, especially for leasing agents.

Q *How were you trained to acquire new clients and retain the loyalty of your current ones?*

I was always told that integrity should always be your strongest suit, and I believe that passionately to this day. You also need for your client to know that you are his or her advocate in the adventure and always have his or her best interest at heart. Nothing can replace repeat business!

Q *Paul, what is your advice about creating and sticking to an annual business plan?*

A business plan is important primarily because it can help you organize your time. In our market there are only so many commercial opportunities that one agent can handle at any given time, unlike a residential agent who can maintain a dozen escrows at once (maybe with a little help), so time management is very important. Making your calls, updating your files, keeping current with your literature, and staying abreast of changes in the marketplace from national to local issues are musts. All these things are important and can be easily pushed aside when you get busy. A business plan is very important because it helps you make the very best use of your time.

Q *What are some key points in the successful preparation for a listing presentation with a prospective seller?*

Being prepared for a commercial listing presentation involves knowing more than the client and more than the competition in terms of other properties on the market, trends in that specialty area, pending rezoning or developments, recent sales or leases, and suggestions for improving the property for a quicker and higher sale. And the client has to be convinced that you will be his advocate throughout the process.

Being prepared for a commercial listing presentation involves knowing more than the client and more than the competition in terms of other properties on the market.

Q *What are the critical steps and/or issues to be thinking about or to cover when you are actually conducting the listing interview with the sellers?*

The first things the seller wants to know are

- How marketable is my property?
- What is it worth?
- What do I need to do to enhance its value and marketability?

In the back of their mind is always whether they will be making any profit on the sale, and how much, but that is often a question they will not openly share with you. The broker's honesty and candor are always the key to his or her credibility; therefore, telling the seller what the market is saying and not necessarily what they may want to hear is sometimes difficult but always critically important. Setting out a marketing plan with accountability built in and time lines is also important.

Writing a commercial purchase contract can be very different than writing a standard residential contract. What are some of the key issues that you feel are important to have covered in the commercial contract?

The commercial contract is always more complicated than the residential contract in that it will often include tenant issues, ownership issues, legal use issues, a lengthy feasibility study or due diligence period with many steps, more complicated lending issues, and a longer escrow closing period. The preprinted forms that most of the real estate associations provide are excellent templates to work from. Some states require an attorney to be involved. The seller and buyer may each have tax issues that need to be addressed to each party's satisfaction and will often require the involvement of their respective tax advisors. The settlement statements will often include prorations of leasehold income, various assessments, prepaid fees, and other items that can make the statements much more complicated. The issuance of the preliminary title report can involve many exclusions that may need to be addressed.

Do you feel that it is wise to have the client's attorney and/or CPA either draft the purchase agreement or, if you draft it, make it contingent on their approval?

In most cases, your client will probably be looking to you to draft the purchase agreement for them, especially in those states where preprinted forms are available or you have a contract form that you have used many times that has been well scrutinized by legal eyes over the years. You are always wise to suggest that your client have their attorney review the contract and to suggest they involve their accountant in any calculations of profit or loss or to help structure the transaction so that it works to the client's advantage from a taxation point of view.

Q *How much should a commercial agent know about Internal Revenue Code Section 1031?*

A good commercial agent should be very familiar with the 1031 tax-deferred exchange provisions of the tax code. Giving your client a good overview of their options is important. Be aware that many accountants have little or no practical knowledge of these provisions, and your client should always ask the accountant if they are familiar with that code section.

A good commercial agent should be very familiar with the 1031 tax-deferred exchange provisions of the tax code.

Q *Tell us your feelings about the value of proper training, mentoring, and guidance.*

Clients can sense insecurity, and if you are not prepared for a meeting with them, then you will probably not do as well as you would have liked. That sense of confidence that all clients desire in their broker comes from a combination of training and preparation. Unfortunately, most communities do not have adequate school training for commercial brokers. And most commercial brokerage firms have done away with the old "mentor" or "runner" systems that produced so many good brokers over the years. That leaves the agent to search out any schooling opportunities they can find on their own.

The CCIM and SIOR [Society of Industrial and Office Realtors®] programs are the ultimate schooling options, but they are expensive and often not conveniently offered. Many community colleges have classes in financial analysis and some of the more academic topics. Some even have real estate programs, but the most important training is always the mentoring, both formal and informal, that we get from our experienced coworkers and competitors. Just doing transactions, whether they are yours or someone in your office who is willing to help, is the surest path to knowledge and self-confidence. If your company does not offer any formal training and there are no experienced agents or managers willing to spend some time with you, then you might think about moving to a more supportive environment.

What are the typical "success patterns" you watch for in a newly developing commercial agent?

The success pattern most common in a new commercial agent is one of wild swings between frantic activity and exasperation. The wild swings are a result of grabbing at anything that smells like it might be a deal and running with it until it runs out. The new commercial agent has not yet developed the sense of "what is real and what is not" that comes from being face-to-face with many clients over the years.

There are always customers wanting to take advantage of a commercial agent's knowledge and information; they will drain him or her dry and give him or her no protection when the deal really comes around, so that agent has just spent untold hours working on something that will never result in a commission check. Having the self-confidence to ask the tough questions needed to "prequalify" a customer comes with time and a few bruises.

The exasperation comes from working on transactions that eventually crash due to activities outside the agent's control—the company changes its plans for a site in the area, or interest rates go up and the corporate finance people don't want to go out that far, or one of the twelve partners dies and their heirs don't want to move forward with the transaction. The number of ways a transaction can go south are endless, but the end result is always an exasperated broker who can never get that time back. The experienced commercial broker can sniff out the real from the unreal and learn to use the protection of either a buyer/broker agreement or an hourly fee format.

Q

Where do you see the commercial market going in the next five to ten years?

Where do you see the commercial market going in the next five to ten years?

The trend is unmistakable in my opinion: easier access to information about properties and easier access to other brokers and buyers and sellers—all through Web-based marketing programs. A good example is the CCIM-sponsored website to do business, but there are others, and there will be more and more over time. The commercial agent of today needs to be comfortable at his or her computer and subscribe to several websites. He or she also needs to be familiar with any of the several desktop publishing programs that are now cheap and easy to use.

Public records are getting more and more accessible online, and the agent's ability to confirm information is getting more convenient for brokers and title companies. That trend will continue for the foreseeable future. The key will remain, as always, controlling the property (getting listings) and/or the buyer. Both of those activities require the personal skills that only a well-trained and -supported commercial agent can provide.

Q

What are the three best tips or pieces of advice you can give to the reader of this book to help him or her to make a decision to enter the commercial real estate field successfully?

1. Do you have the temperament to deal with failure and rejection on a fairly regular basis and keep optimistic and positive? The percent of commercial transactions that actually close and fund is considerably less than in residential sales, so time will be spent that is not rewarded by a successful closing, time and again.

2. Do you have the financial resources to sustain yourself and perhaps your family for many months with no commissions coming in? The single most intense pressure is that which comes from the financial stress of not having a predictable

income stream. It is much more difficult to create an "income rhythm" in commercial real estate because the escrows are usually so much longer and the "times at bat" are fewer.

3. Do you enjoy being with people? The most successful real estate people are those who are working all the time. By that, I mean their work is so integrated into the rest of their lives that there is no clear division between working and not working. If you can get to the point where you are enjoying being with your clients and customers regardless of the time of day, your success will be assured.

Kenneth Young
Managing Director—Leasing
Equity Office Properties
San Francisco, California
Leasing

> **Ken, tell the readers about yourself. How and when did you get into real estate?**

I got into real estate in 1984 not long after graduating from college. The local market was just beginning to flourish at that time (i.e., the office-building boom for San Mateo County). I was fortunate in that Grubb & Ellis had an entry-level program in the fledgling area of research.

> **What made you decide on commercial versus residential real estate, and how did you decide on a career in commercial leasing?**

I never really considered a career in the residential arena. I did not (and do not) believe I had the temperament and approach necessary to be successful in the residential field. My assessment, which I still believe to be correct, was that the residential market is more "emotional" than that of the business world. People tend to be significantly more invested in their homes than their workplace (which is not to say people are not keenly interested in where they work—it's just different). As to why commercial real estate: I had noted over time that many wealthy people became that way as a result of real estate investment and involvement. Prior to the tech boom, in which so many people created wealth, real estate was the best vehicle to becoming affluent.

> **What are some of the biggest issues you face as a leasing specialist (ADA, tenant bankruptcy, etc.)?**

The greatest challenges in the commercial field involve the day-to-day matters in the transactions and also the long-term strategy required to stay at the forefront of the market and industry. Another key challenge is working and dealing with local municipalities. Unfortunately, each city works differently, and it can be extremely frustrating trying to absorb and comply with the way each city handles planning and permits. When you couple the constantly changing environment (due to personnel changes) and the subjective way in which municipalities apply the building code, you have a recipe for exasperation.

Q *Does your firm specialize in leasing only one type of property, and if so, what type?*

Equity Office Properties is primarily an owner and operator of Class A office buildings in various major metropolitan areas (e.g., Boston, New York, Chicago, Denver, Austin, San Francisco, Portland, and Seattle) and certain suburbs of these metropolitan areas.

Q *What are the unique issues you face with leasing that type of property versus other income-producing properties?*

There are typically higher costs associated in the re-lease of office property. Other types of commercial real estate (e.g., retail and industrial) do not incur the higher costs associated with improving their spaces. Retail is often delivered in a "vanilla shell"—that is, ready for the retail entity to perform their own improvements. Industrial properties are often leased for their utility (i.e., dock-high loading, truck staging, warehouse ceiling clear height, etc.). As such, there tends to be greater risk associated with office buildings because of the capital outlay necessary, barring an extraordinarily strong market where landlords can push much if not all of the improvement costs to the customer.

> *There are typically higher costs associated in the re-lease of office property.*

Q *Does your firm do property management as well? If so, is that a separate division, or is it all under one division?*

We do indeed manage our own properties, which I believe to be the best approach. Not to take anything away from the many excellent third-party property management firms in the industry, but I believe there is pride of ownership in first-party management that cannot be replicated by a third party given the typical demands and situations of third-party management.

Our firm does indeed separate the leasing functions from the property management functions. This segregated approach allows people to truly excel in their given discipline and not get bogged down in a jack-of-all-trades scenario. While there is certainly merit in having a finger in all pies, I do not believe one can be completely effective if actively involved and engaged in the complementary functions. Because of this separation of responsibilities, it is extremely critical for us to communicate effectively and *constantly*.

How and when do you and your group create an annual business plan? How often do you meet to assess your performance against the business plan?

We create our business plan, if you will, beginning in July of the preceding calendar year. At that point we assess the activity in the market (using our experiences and information from the brokerage and business communities) and project, to the best we can, the demand, leasing velocity, and basic economics of transaction and when they may occur. This involves some "crystal balling," as is likely to be in projections of this nature. We review this plan again in the fourth quarter of the preceding year and then again in each quarter of the affected period. Fact is, we really evaluate matters on a day-to-day basis as the market evolves and reveals itself.

Will you explain what you mean by leasing velocity?

Will you explain what you mean by leasing velocity?

Leasing velocity, as I refer to it, is simply the rate at which space is getting leased. As you might imagine, leasing velocity tends to be greater in good or improving markets. Velocity may be increased to a certain extent by creating the spaces that are in highest demand at any given time (e.g., 1,000 to 4,000 square feet in our San Francisco Peninsula market). These spaces are typically created by speculative demising larger spaces. While capital is put at risk by improving the spaces ahead of a lease or even a prospect, it is generally prudent if the created space is functional for the general user.

How do you interface with the brokerage agents?

The vast majority of our business is procured through the brokerage community, and we recognize the value they contribute in the transaction process. Our interactions are on a daily basis whether through a deal or just a warm call to see how things are going or to solicit an opinion on an initiative we are contemplating. We recognize that whatever we do in the market—whether it is raising our rates or implementing a new leasing program or incentive—the brokers are our best resource.

Does your firm do any selling or are you strictly leasing?

The core of our company's business is leasing office space.

How many leasing agents are employed at your firm, and how much area does your branch office cover?

On the San Francisco Peninsula, we have three deal makers (including me) who cover the approximately 4.7 million square feet in the subregion, which spans from San Bruno in the north to Palo Alto in the south—all in all, fifty-four buildings. As a company, we have approximately 125 dealmakers in the Leasing group.

Are your leasing agents on salary, or are they commission based?

The compensation structure varies from person to person, but generally it is a base salary with a bonus component.

Q *Does your firm conduct leasing activities for a portfolio group of investment owners, or do you seek new business from other building owners in the area?*

As mentioned earlier, we are only involved with buildings we own either in total or in joint venture with various financial partners.

Q *What effect does the economy have on your business, if any?*

As the economy goes, so goes commercial real estate, not unlike so many other businesses. Office buildings do better in an expanding economy since that typically means job growth for which companies need more office space.

Q *Do you hire agents who are new to real estate, residential agents wanting a change of career within the industry, or only experienced leasing agents?*

We tend to want people with deal-making experience prior to joining the leasing group. It is not to say that we do not "bring people up through the ranks," but with our structure, it works best with experienced people from the community.

Q *What type of new agent training do you offer?*

Since we are not a traditional brokerage house, we do not have the typical programs that you may find in the brokerage community. However, we are constantly training our people in technology, sales skills, and, most importantly, customer service. We strongly believe that customer service is the number one element in a successful business.

Q

So your training is the same for new agents and veterans alike, except that new agents are put into some type of mentor program?

That's right.

Q

Residential real estate experiences a very high turnover with as many as 85 percent of new licensees leaving the business within three years. How high is the turnover in commercial leasing?

We have a propensity to have people work with us for extended periods of time. While real estate does indeed tend to be a transient business, our core group of leasing professionals remains intact year after year.

Q

If an experienced residential agent or a new licensee came to you and said, "I want to become a leasing specialist," what advice would you give him or her?

Have your head examined! Seriously, though, I would encourage them to do their homework about the industry; that is, talk to as many people as they could within the industry, those with varying levels of tenure and experience. Essentially, "gather the cards" and make a critical assessment as to whether the field matches up with their objectives.

Q

What are the three best pieces of advice you would give to someone embarking on a career in commercial leasing?

1. Be organized and methodical. Really plan your approach to the business by setting realistic but high goals that can be achieved but monitored and adjusted accordingly.

2. Be a student of the business; read as many business-related magazines and articles as possible, not just about real estate but about business in general, including emerging industries and so forth.

3. Network—let friends, family, and others know what you are doing and how you can be of assistance.

4. I know you asked for three but here is one more: *do not be afraid of the word* no *because you will hear it often. Learn how to deal with it constructively.*

Is there anything I have missed that you would like to tell the person reading this book about succeeding in commercial leasing?

Yes. Try to gain an understanding and appreciation for both sides of the business, the landlord and the tenant. With that appreciation should come an understanding of the terms and conditions of most leases and what each condition means to the respective parties. Generally there will be commonality in most leases, especially those of an "institutional" nature such as properties owned by REITs, insurance companies, large-scale ("nonpublic") companies, pension funds, and entities such as that.

Don't just be an "order taker" with clients. Act as a true consultant and not a yes man. Too often, brokers—especially younger ones—tend to fear their clients and are thus unduly influenced in how they comport themselves in a transaction. This is a disservice to the clients, the brokers, and the agent himself or herself. To combat this tendency, be prepared to discuss the market vis-à-vis the clients' requirements, in a realistic fashion using unbiased information. If a client is being unreasonable in actions and expectations, do not be afraid to respectfully withdraw from representing them as a client.

> *If a client is being unreasonable in actions and expectations, do not be afraid to respectfully withdraw from representing them as a client.*

While it may seem painful, especially as you are building your client base, you and your reputation will benefit in the long run. You will not lose credibility with your peers and associates, as may be the case when representing "nightmare clients," and you will not run the risk of wasting your valuable time, which is one of the major challenges in establishing your business practice. In short, only work with motivated and qualified client opportunities.

Work with clients who are committed to you in their search for leasing opportunities. It allows you time to be focused on their needs and will not result in the panic that typically results from a client who "works with everybody."

Be professionally aggressive in your pursuit of business. Nobody ever made it big in brokerage by "hoping and waiting" by the phone. Such a passive approach will result in certain failure.

Never give legal advice to your clients. Always strongly encourage them to engage legal counsel when entering into a lease. The same thing goes for tax advice or any advice outside the scope of the broker.

Follow up in writing; whether it is a thank-you note or a confirmation of a conversation. This is one of the greatest things about e-mail—the availability of immediate written communication. Acting in this fashion helps avoid the "he said, she said" situations when you are negotiating and implementing a lease.

Never ever take someone at their word when it comes to something not included in the lease document that should have been there. All material elements should be in writing in the lease document.

Be honest and act with integrity at all times. Nothing is more valuable to you than your good reputation.

Do not apologize for what you do and how much money you make. Commercial real estate brokerage can be very lucrative, and brokers are often accused of being overcompensated and, as such, are reviled. Ignore such statements, or respond in good humor.

Mark Schneider
Coldwell Banker Residential Brokerage
Tucson, Arizona
Property Management

Note: Mark was formerly General Manager of IBM's Executive Conference Center in New York and worked as a Senior Property Manager for Grubb & Ellis Commercial Brokerage.

Mark, tell the readers about you. How and when did you get into real estate?

It was 1982, and I was the general manager of IBM's Executive Conference Center in New York. This position gave me exposure to many of IBM's top executives, and it was there I first met IBM's Real Estate and Construction president, Jack Williams. Mr. Williams was speaking about the importance of real estate to the corporation and the need for increased manufacturing capacity and space to house the tens of thousands of employees IBM was hiring at the time. At this time IBM was ramping up to increase its capacity—buying land, building manufacturing facilities, and adding leased space for sales and marketing. [The year] 1982 was part of the go-go days at IBM, and we all worked hard to meet the demand for increased capacity and size.

What made you decide on commercial property management instead of residential real estate?

I joined IBM's Real Estate and Construction Division (RECD) as a leasing specialist. My territory was the state of New York, and I had heard a rumor that there might be a few sharks swimming around in that real estate pool. I was new and felt like a ship out of water.

As a leasing specialist, my job was to service the existing leases and add or cancel leases based on the space needs of the IBM sites in New York. Bob, I was really concerned about the New York real estate sharks, and I was determined not to get eaten alive in my first transaction. So, with little background and training, I set out to learn as much as I could as fast as I could. I also asked for a mentor, someone I could go to for advice and expertise. I read everything I could get my hands on, attended classes, and frequently asked my mentor and other senior leasing specialists for advice. It was survival of the fittest.

What were some of the biggest issues you faced as a property management specialist (Americans with Disabilities Act, tenant bankruptcy, portfolio management, obtaining new properties to manage, etc.)?

Part of the excitement and challenge of property management is that there is always a myriad of issues and personalities to deal with, and you usually don't know which one will pop up next. The keys to success are anticipation and being quick on your feet. My first day in property management, I asked the seasoned "old-timer" property manager whom I was replacing, "What are the keys to success as a property manager?" I'll never forget his answer to my question. He said, "Keep the building comfortable—not too hot, not too cold. Keep it clean, and do repairs promptly."

Understanding and interpreting ADA (Americans with Disabilities Act) was a huge challenge when it first became law. It took the industry and corporations a while to understand all the regulations and requirements. Initially the regulations were very confusing and expensive to implement. Many facilities required extensive work and a significant budget to meet ADA's new regulations. Tenant bankruptcy and portfolio management are all important property management issues because they both affect a building's income stream.

What are the unique issues you face while managing office buildings?

Managing office buildings is quite different from managing other types of income-producing properties. Managing a multitenant building with over two thousand people is like being the mayor of a small city trying to keep different parties and all the inhabitants (voters?) happy and content. Your days are usually filled with not only property and repair issues but people issues that are sometimes rational but at times very emotional as well.

Q *Did your firm do leasing as well? If so, was that a separate division, or was it all under one division?*

I have been with several companies and experienced leasing both ways. When leasing was an integral part of the property management division, communications were improved, and I think everyone felt more like a team. Typically in many large commercial real estate firms, leasing is either organizationally separate or is physically distant on a separate floor.

Q *How and when did you and your group create an annual business plan? How often did you meet to assess your performance against the business plan?*

Every company, small or large, must plan and measure their performance if they expect to be successful. While the methodology is slightly different from firm to firm, the need and importance of developing good business plans and accurately tracking the group's financial performance are keys to the success of the organization. This really applies to every individual as well, if you really think about it.

Most annual planning takes place in the fourth quarter of the year. Generally, finance would send a set of financial assumptions that we were required to follow. However, the bottom line is that the budget and the assumptions both have to be realistic and based only on very accurate year-to-date (YTD) and last month's information. As a property manager, you really have to be able to interpret both recent and historical financial information. Certain items are predictable and hit you every month, while others are less predictable and can vary by thousands of dollars, severely affecting not only the budget but your ability to continue operations. Failure to allow for contingency planning can literally wipe you out.

Our planning process was always to get the most recent twelve months of the operating results. Then we would go through each budget line item by line item in an attempt to examine and understand what was included and what might not be included and thus a liability for next year. The key to making a good and accurate forecast is accurate input. After the budget was inputted, it was reviewed for compliance to budget criteria, and at times we were asked by finance to reduce expenditures.

Measurements were monthly. The best measurement system I saw and the one I still use today measures the following:

- Current month this year versus same month last year
- Current YTD versus last year YTD
- Current month versus budget
- YTD versus YTD budget

Any significant variance should be reviewed in depth, and any exposures to the plan should be reported. I always found if you were going to miss your plan, it was best to tell upper management early rather than surprise them at the end of the year.

How did you interface with the brokerage agents?

Most of the time interaction between brokers and property management occurred at branch offices, account meetings, socially, or at the water cooler.

How many property management agents did Grubb & Ellis employ when you were there, and how much area did your branch cover?

Grubb & Ellis employed hundreds of property managers nationally. As a portfolio manager, I managed over twenty-two property managers at various sites throughout six Southwest states.

Were you salaried or on commission?

For the majority of my career I was salaried. However, within the salary structure, I usually had provisions that typically allowed for bonus incentives of 20 percent to 50 percent of my salary.

Q *Did Grubb & Ellis conduct property management activities for a portfolio group of investment owners, or did you seek new business from other building owners in your area?*

Grubb & Ellis was always on the lookout for new business opportunities or to expand with our existing clients.

Q *What effect does the economy have on property management, if any?*

Commercial real estate ownership is generally viewed as a long-term commitment and therefore a strategic decision for most businesses. Therefore, almost all decisions are made only after a thorough business analysis and in-depth planning.

The economy impacts commercial real estate much as it does other areas of business. Effects can be immediate. Good news about the economy brings optimism and expansion that result in signed leases, while bad news can result in vacant space. That's why leasing commissions are based only on signed leases.

When I worked for IBM, our strategic plan was to have a diversity of commitments for all our real estate holdings. Manufacturing plants and holdings in major cities were usually company owned, and we generally entered into long-term leased office space for sales and marketing in the major cities. We did shorter leases in the smaller cities. That strategy was implemented so we could flex our space up or down according to the economy.

Q *Did you hire agents new to real estate, residential agents wanting a change of career within the industry, or only experienced leasing agents?*

I hired property managers with and without experience based on their overall qualifications and ability to communicate effectively.

What type of new agent training did your company offer?

I've been around for quite a while now and experienced all forms of training. When I was hired, I was assigned a mentor who guided me through my first transactions. This was supplemented by training NACORE, IDRC, BOMA, IFMA, and classes at the Wharton School of Business.

What type of ongoing training did your firm offer its existing staff?

Ongoing training came in two ways. In-house from seasoned professionals was conducted two to four times a year, and we had professional training from outside agencies on and off. We were usually allowed to take an outside course once a year.

Residential real estate experiences a very high turnover, with as many as 85 percent of new licensees leaving the business within three years. How high is the turnover in commercial property management?

Commercial real estate requires a much larger investment in time and training. As a consequence, the hiring process for commercial real estate agents is much more stringent and in depth. Large commercial firms are looking for highly qualified candidates, often with MBA degrees or real estate or a related undergraduate degree. Consequently, the turnover in commercial real estate is much lower than it is for residential.

If an experienced residential real estate agent or new licensee came to you and said, "I want to go into property management," what advice would you give that person?

Before I could offer any advice, I would have to know the individual's motivation for such a career change. Depending on their motives, I would offer some advice. Basically, for someone who has a successful career in residential real estate, I would ask, "Why do you want to start over?" In cases dealing with those new to real estate, I would just like to make sure they have the right motivation, and they are not thinking it's easier and they'll make thousands of dollars more.

What are the three best pieces of advice you would give to someone embarking on a career in commercial property management?

I would tell them the following:

1. As a property manager, learn the basics and execute them. Keep the buildings comfortable and in good shape.

2. Maintain your buildings within the budget.

3. Sharpen your marketing skills, build relationships, and thoroughly educate yourself in your industry.

4. Understand there is no easy way to the millions other than marrying the boss's daughter.

Is there anything else I missed about succeeding in commercial property management that you would like to tell the person reading this book?

Bob, I'm sure you know from writing several books on real estate that it is hard to sum up what you have learned over many years into just a few words, but here it is. Commercial real estate is like most other professions: it can be rewarding and lucrative, or it can be a frustrating daily grind. I believe the key to success is in the approach. If you approach commercial real estate thinking it's easy money, you'll soon be discouraged. However, if you want to get into commercial real estate because you like working with people, enjoy solving problems, and are willing to work hard, you can enjoy a good career and make very good money.

14

Success Patterns of High-Producing Commercial Agents

*I*n this chapter, I asked several very successful commercial agents whom I know personally to give me their three or four best tips for succeeding in commercial real estate. I asked them, "If a new agent or an experienced residential agent came to you and said they were going into commercial real estate, what advice would you give them?"

Here are their answers.

Harvey Mordka

Broker/owner of Harvey Mordka Realty, Tucson, Arizona

35 years' experience

1. Fear and trepidation

   "Fear of the unknown has kept many a person from pursuing an area of interest. Everyone seems to know and be pretty comfortable with the residential side of the business. Commercial seems to hold a fascination of bigger-ticket sales but comes with higher risk and higher potential liability. If you genuinely have an interest in doing commercial sales or leasing, then you need to set your fears aside and go on to tips 2 through 4."

   If you genuinely have an interest in doing commercial sales or leasing, then you need to set your fears aside.

2. Educate yourself

   "Many people have a desire to do things but don't want to pay the price of educating themselves in the commercial arena. It's a commitment of time and money."

3. Commitment to success

   "Once you have eliminated the fear and have obtained the education, you are ready to commit to the daily activities of being successful. Technology has come a long way, but there is still the value of personalization. Seeing the people eyeball to eyeball and building personal relationships is invaluable to being successful. Your commitment to serving the buyers' and sellers' needs will reward you financially and with repeat and referral business in the future."

4. Specialization versus generalization

   "Each of us has a niche that we are comfortable in. Find what and where you are happiest and pursue that area. Do not be afraid to take risks and learn new territory to travel. We are blessed to live in a country that is only 230 years old. Look how far we have come as a nation. From a landing on the East Coast, being hunters and gatherers, farming, manufacturing, inventing, developing, railroads, airplanes, cars, arts/theater, sports venues, rural and urban parks, and more! Under all is the land! What share of the commercial market would you like?"

Gary Best, CCIM

Associate Broker with Realty Executives Southern Arizona

Former president of the Tucson Association of REALTORS®

36 years' experience

The single most important characteristic of success in commercial real estate and actually in any endeavor where high achievement is possible is commitment.

"OK, Bob, here goes: The single most important characteristic of success in commercial real estate and actually in any endeavor where high achievement is possible is *commitment,* far and away more than any other characteristic. I am reminded of two top world-class athletes: Seven-time Tour de France Champion Lance Armstrong and Kerri Strug, from Tucson, who won Olympic gold for her and her team in the 1996 Olympics. Both have acknowledged pain in their journeys, probably more than they acknowledged, but the strength of their commitment to doing the very best they could do is what sustained their efforts, especially at the very last moments of their respective competitions.

"The mastery of certain processes also goes a long way toward success, particularly in commercial real estate. Different words can be used and presented differently in various businesses, but these processes are, not necessarily in order of importance:

- Thinking creatively
- Communicating effectively
- Organizing one's selling efforts
- Management of time
- Ability to overcome objections
- Staying motivated

"Much has been written about these skills as applied to any goal-oriented environment, but they are critical. The application of these skills, while never perfect, will determine the level of success any person or group of people will be able to achieve. The *commitment* must be strong, as the adversity to achievement of worthy goals will certainly be strong. As I considered your question, I kept coming back to these basics again and again."

Maureen Vosburgh
Coldwell Banker Residential Brokerage

21 years' experience

"I joined an independent commercial firm in Hartford, Connecticut, when I first started in the mid-1980s. I was told I shouldn't plan on any closed transactions for at least two years. As fate would have it, by the end of my first year in the business I was responsible for the largest commercial sale ($28,500,000) in the company's history and became the number one agent in the entire company. I did it despite the fact that I was one of only two women in a company that was dominated by over twenty men and tremendous sexism. The general market was 'good old boy' through and through.

"Why was I successful?

- I listened to my clients and really focused on their needs.

- I cultivated my very first client who, with his two partners, bought a small historic building from me. The same threesome joined with seven partners in two other firms to form a still-larger company. It was that group that bought the historic office building for $28,500,000.

- I communicated well with all of my clients (especially those ten). I kept in constant touch.

- I had many more commercial transactions, including several more with the original 'cast of ten,' and I remain close friends with my original contact, who now lives in Maine."

Debbie Green

Long Realty Co.

18 years' experience

"Bob, as you know, I specialize in land brokerage, so my comments are confined to that area. A good agent needs to look past the obvious, so here are the three top things an agent should look for when representing someone in a land transaction:

- Identify zoning in writing from the proper municipalities—and record the name of the person you talked to.

- Look for any deed recorded restrictions that could alter the zoning.

- Ask questions of the sellers. Have they ever been involved in or know of any legal judgments, claims, liens, and so forth, that have occurred that may alter the use by the next owner?

  Ask questions of the sellers.

- Look for recorded judgments that limit the use of the land that the sellers may be trying to hide (it's happened!).

15

Property Management

Property management has become a very specialized field, with some firms specializing in residential income properties while others only manage retail shopping centers, office buildings, or some other type of commercial property.

Most owners do not want to become involved with the day-to-day management of their commercial real estate investments; instead, they employ the services of a professional firm to oversee them. This is often advisable from a legal standpoint as well as an operational one. Many laws must be adhered to, such as the Americans with Disabilities Act and fair housing issues. Serious commercial property owners usually want the added benefit of a professional manager handling compliance with these and other legal issues.

Serious commercial property owners usually want the added benefit of a professional manager handling compliance with these and other legal issues.

The Institute of Real Estate Management (IREM) awards the professional designation of Accredited Management Organization (AMO) to a company that meets the following standards:

- At least one Certified Property Manager (CPM) in charge
- Annual accreditation renewal
- Adherence to minimum standards and the rules set by IREM
- Property management as a primary activity

Many property management firms specialize only in condominium association management. These firms collect homeowner association dues, send newsletters, hold the required annual meetings, enforce sanctions against homeowners who violate rules, prepare tax returns, and handle worker's compensation and insurance claims. Virtually all property management firms work under a management agreement whereby the firm is empowered with specific duties and obligations on behalf of the property owner. The three types of property managers include the following:

- *Licensed property manager.* This person is a licensed real estate agent employed by a real estate firm that manages property or an individual broker who manages property for others for a fee. Persons working under the direct supervision of a licensed property manager need not be licensed.

- *Individual property manager.* This person manages a single property for an owner and may or may not be a real estate licensee. This is usually a salaried position and may or may not include free use of one of the building's rental units.

- *Resident manager.* A resident manager lives on the premises and may be employed by the owner or a property management firm. This person usually has special training or previous experience and the type of personality that lends itself to dealing well with tenants. Some necessary traits include these:

  Sales skills necessary to "show and sell" the rental units

  Computer and data analysis skills

  The ability to identify problematic maintenance issues and ensure the proper and timely care of the property

  A "take-charge" attitude and a high degree of confidence

  Accuracy in handling bookkeeping duties, money, and bank deposits

  A keen sense of what is happening on the premises and in the area

  The ability to select residents based on credit reports and personal references

  Ability to make timely and accurate reports

State-Defined Responsibilities

A property manager who is licensed as a real estate professional must act in a fiduciary capacity as the agent of the owner. State licensing laws charge each property manager with a list of specific duties, which include the following:

State licensing laws charge each property manager with a list of specific duties.

- Paying insurance premiums and taxes and recommending tax appeals when warranted

- Establishing the rental schedule that will bring the highest yield consistent with good economics

- Keeping abreast of economic and competitive market conditions

- Merchandising the space and collecting the rents

- Frequently inspecting vacant space

- Creating and supervising maintenance schedules and repairs

- Planning alterations and modernizing programs

- Supervising all purchasing

- Advertising and publicizing vacancies through selected media and broker lists

- Developing a policy for landlord-tenant relations

- Auditing and paying bills

- Maintaining proper records and making regular reports to the owner

- Hiring, instructing, and maintaining satisfactory personnel to staff the building(s)

- Qualifying and investigating prospective tenants' credit

- Preparing decorating specifications and securing estimates

- Preparing and executing leases

Specific Duties

Under a property management agreement, the manager assumes all executive
functions of the owner and is fully in
charge of the details connected with the
operation and physical upkeep of the
property.

A conscientious manager is responsible
for the following:

*Under a property
management
agreement, the
manager assumes
all executive
functions of the
owner.*

- Handling residents' questions promptly and properly

- Never denying a resident's request without clearly stating why

- Advising renters what is expected of them and what they can
  expect from the owner (this should be in writing as a matter of
  policy)

- Treating residents fairly and sympathetically

- Using care to protect the tenants' and prospective tenants' legal
  rights with regard to fair housing and ADA issues, and so
  forth.

Establishing Rent Schedules

The law of supply and demand in an area dictates the amount set for
rents. To set proper rent schedules, the manager must make a thorough
analysis of the neighborhood and immediate area. The analysis should
include but not be limited to

- Current area vacancy factors;

- Availability of transportation, recreation, churches, and schools
  and proximity to shopping;

- Trends in population growth and occupants per unit;

- The character, age, and condition of the immediate
  neighborhood;

- The financial ability and size of families in the immediate
  area;

- Directional growth of the community and the economic health of local businesses;

- The condition of the housing market versus population growth trends.

The objective of good property management is to achieve a level of rent and vacancy that provides the highest net return to the property owner. Conducting regular rental surveys and establishing competitive rent schedules is primary to this objective. Bad tenants who use and often abuse a property while not paying rent are worse than having a vacant unit. The only competition a vacant unit has is other vacant units, not rented units.

The objective of good property management is to achieve a level of rent and vacancy that provides the highest net return to the property owner.

Accounting Records

Although the number of bookkeeping records needed depends on the type of property managed and the volume of business involved, the selection and maintenance of an adequate trust account system is essential in property management due to the fiduciary nature of the business.

The property management broker is charged with the responsibility of trust fund recordkeeping. An annual audit by an outside accounting firm is highly recommended.

The following are reasons for keeping accounting records:

- The law states that a separate record must be kept for each managed property.

- They provide the broker with a source of information when problems arise or an inquiry is made.

- They are necessary for income tax purposes.

- They serve as controls in analyzing costs, preparing budgets, and evaluating income and expenses.

- Contractual relations and the Business and Professions Code mandate a complete and accurate accounting of all funds.

- They are required for full disclosure and accounting to third parties with an interest in the property.

- The fiduciary relationship between the owner and the manager dictates full disclosure.

A property manager must be fully aware of both the landlord's and tenants' responsibilities.

Tenant's Responsibilities

According to the civil code of most states, a tenant must do the following:

- Keep the living unit clean and sanitary.
- Use all utility fixtures properly.
- Use the property only for its intended lawful purpose.
- Pay rent on time.
- Dispose of garbage and other waste in a sanitary manner.
- Abide by all rules and regulations.
- Give a written thirty-day notice when vacating.
- Return door and mailbox keys when vacating.
- Leave the unit in a clean condition when vacating.

Landlord's Responsibilities

A residential lease has an implied warranty of habitability. This does not extend to issues caused by a lack of tenant cleanliness. The landlord must keep the property in reasonably good order and repair, including the plumbing, heating, electrical systems, and all areas under the landlord's care. The roof must be kept free of leaks, and all health and safety issues (e.g., loose railings) should be addressed in a reasonable time frame.

If the landlord allows the property to fall into a state of *uninhabitable* disrepair or the property becomes uninhabitable due to health and safety issues, the landlord cannot collect any rent. Violating this may subject the landlord and/or the property manager to actual and special damages from the tenants. A tenant can also raise the defense of habitability against an eviction notice.

If a landlord fails to make a timely correction of a repair that is his or her responsibility, the tenant has three options:

1. The tenant may abandon the property and not be held liable for back rents or an unfulfilled lease.

2. The tenant may refer the problem to a mediator, an arbitrator, or, for serious problems, small claims court.

3. The tenant may notify the owner in writing of an emergency situation that must be taken care of. If the owner fails to respond, the tenant may call his or her own repair people and offset the repair costs with up to one month's rent on the next rent check. States impose a maximum number of times this may be used by a tenant in each year of tenancy, so check with your local and state about this issue. In many states, a tenant cannot be prohibited from installing a satellite dish within the area under the tenant's control, so check with your local and state authorities about this issue as well.

Assignment versus Sublease

A tenant has the right to assign or sublease his or her interest in a property unless the lease specifically prohibits it.

An assignment transfers the entire leasehold rights to a third party. The third party pays his or her rent directly to the original lessor, and the original lessee is eliminated.

A sublease of property transfers only a part of a tenant's interest. The sublessee pays his or her rent to the original lessee, who in turn is still responsible for payment of rent to the lessor. The original lessee has what is referred to as a "sandwich lease."

A lease should clearly indicate whether or not it may be assigned or subleased. Leases often state that no subletting or assignment shall take place without the express written permission of the lessor, which shall not be unreasonably withheld.

Termination of a Lease

A tenancy for a specified period, such as an estate for years, requires no notice of termination because the date has already been specified. A month-to-month tenancy necessitates a written thirty-day notice because of its perpetual existence. It is always a good idea for a tenant to give a landlord a written notice in any event.

Evictions and Unlawful Detainer Actions

A landlord may evict a tenant and bring an unlawful detainer action against him or her for failure to pay rent when due, violations of provisions contained in the lease or rental agreement, or failure to vacate the premises after termination of thirty days' written notice. Removing a tenant for nonpayment of rent entails the following process:

1. The landlord serves the tenant with a three-day notice to pay or quit the premises.

2. If the tenant fails to heed the notice, the landlord files an unlawful detainer action in municipal court.

3. If the landlord wins, the court awards the landlord a judgment. The landlord then asks for a writ of possession authorizing the sheriff to evict the tenant.

4. The sheriff sends the tenant an eviction notice. If the tenant fails to leave, the sheriff then physically removes the tenant.

Many state legislatures have authorized city attorneys and prosecutor offices to bring unlawful detainer actions to abate drug-related nuisances. The landlord is charged fees and costs.

If a small claims court action is necessary to recoup money from a tenant for lost rent or property damage, an owner or property manager may do so without the aid of an attorney. The maximum amount is the amount set by the small claims court.

Retaliatory Eviction

In some states, a landlord cannot decrease services, increase rent, or evict a tenant within 180 days after the tenant exercises a right protected under the law, including:

- Lawfully organizing a tenant association,

- Complaining to a landlord about the habitability of the premises, or

- Complaining to a public agency about property defects.

A tenant cannot waive his or her rights against retaliatory eviction.

Prohibition of retaliatory eviction is a defense against eviction. If a landlord has been shown to have acted maliciously, the tenant is entitled to actual damages and punitive damages as set by local or state law.

16

Commercial Leasing

A primary responsibility of a property manager is leasing property or acting as a consultant in the drafting of a lease. While most property management firms also draft leases on behalf of the owners whose properties are under their care, some property management firms rely on companies that specialize in leasing property only, and they do not get involved with any other part of property management. This type of arrangement is usually limited to large portfolio-sized holdings that call for very specialized knowledge of certain types of leases, such as very large high-rise office buildings with long-term leases.

When a lease is created, the owner is the *lessor* and the tenant is the *lessee*. A leasehold estate arises when an owner or a property manager acting as the owner's agent grants a tenant the right to occupy the owner's property for a specified period of time for a valuable consideration.

Antidiscrimination

Rigid antidiscrimination issues must be dealt with properly. However, a leasing agent can discriminate against a tenant for legitimate reasons such as bad credit, late rent payments at a prior rental, *Rigid antidiscrimination issues must be dealt with properly.* noted property damage, or bankruptcy. When conducting leasing activities on behalf of nonresidential properties such as office buildings, restaurants, ministorage units, and so on, the leasing agent must be very careful not to violate the Americans with Disabilities Act (ADA).

Leasing agents are under no obligation to accept a bad tenant; it is easier to turn these people down than it is to evict them. Leasing agents may usually charge a nonrefundable screening fee, and the amount that may be charged is usually set by state law. This fee is to cover the cost of gathering information about a prospective tenant to make a decision about renting to him or her.

Note: The method of screening prospective tenants must be uniform in nature to avoid being charged with discriminatory rental screening practices.

> *The method of screening prospective tenants must be uniform in nature to avoid being charged with discriminatory rental screening practices.*

Lease Provisions

Although leases for less than one year may be verbal in some states, a good leasing agent will get *all* leases in writing, including short-term vacation property rental leases. A written lease has the effect of putting all of the agreed-on terms and conditions in writing for the mutual protection of all parties, including the brokers. If leasing a property that is subject to rules and regulations, attach them as a rider to the lease and have the tenant sign for them.

Don't try to draft a lease or use a "cut-and-paste" method of assembling a lease as this may create errors and omissions that would probably be considered the unlawful practice of law. It is best to use the forms available through your local MLS for simple leases and month-to-month rental agreements and obtain the services of a real estate attorney for more complex leases, especially those of a commercial nature.

Names of the Parties

A lease must contain the full names of all parties. A lease to a party who is under the age of eighteen requires a cosigner unless the underage party can prove he or she is an *emancipated minor* by reason of marriage or court order. It would be best to check with your attorney with regard to this matter. The parties must sign the lease *"jointly and severally,"* so that each party to the lease is liable for the entire rent, and you can look to one or all of the tenants for payment.

Dates

The lease must have a beginning and an ending date.

Description of the Premises

The demised premises must be described in such a way that there is no ambiguity. If a storage room, garage, or parking space is included, it should be clearly stated in writing. A lease for office space should state the approximate square footage and the unit number if possible.

Rent and Late Charge

The amount of rent and where and when it is due must be clearly stated. A provision must be made for a late charge if the rent is not received by a specified time on or after its due date. The late charge should not exceed the amount (usually expressed as a percentage of the rent) mandated by the laws of your state to avoid having it deemed too high and declared as unenforceable penalty.

Waterbeds

Common waterbed agreements require the tenant to pay for a policy of waterbed insurance and use a waterbed liner.

Pets

Pet agreements are common in residential leases. They usually restrict the size and/or number of pets. A higher cleaning fee is usually charged to tenants with pets.

Inspection of the Premises

Some leases provide for pretenancy and end-of-tenancy walk-through inspections. Deficiencies must be noted on a form provided for this purpose, which must be signed by the tenant and landlord or property manager.

Cleaning and Security Deposits

A security deposit functions as an insurance policy for the landlord in the event the premises are left damaged or dirty or if rent is owed. While nonrefundable *cleaning deposits* are not allowed in many states, a landlord may charge a security deposit in an amount set by the laws of each state. For instance, in California, a security deposit equal to two months' rent may be charged for an unfurnished unit and up to three months' rent for a furnished unit.

When the tenant vacates, the landlord is only allowed to retain as much of the tenant's deposit as is reasonably necessary to remedy tenant defaults. Any unused portion of the deposit must be returned to the tenant at his or her last known address within three weeks after the premises are vacated. Again, check your state laws regarding this time limit because it may vary. Failure of the landlord to comply with this statute may make him or her liable to the tenant through a small claims court action, an attorney, or a complaint filed by the tenant through the Consumer Protection Bureau.

Exculpatory Clause

Leases frequently contain an exculpatory clause (hold-harmless clause) whereby the tenant relieves the landlord of any and all liability for personal injury or property damage that results from the owner's negligence or the condition of the property. These clauses are usually invalid in residential leases, even if the tenant has agreed to one of them, and his or her legal rights are still intact.

Right of Entry

Most leases contain a provision that allows the landlord to enter the premises for specific purposes. If a lease is lacking such a provision, the landlord can enter only when

- An emergency requires entry;
- The tenant consents to an entry;
- The tenant has surrendered or abandoned the premises;
- The landlord has obtained a court order permitting entry;
- The entry is during normal business hours after reasonable notice (this time will vary by state, so get to know yours) to make necessary and or agreed-on repairs, alterations, or improvements, or to show the premises to prospective or actual purchasers, mortgagees, tenants, workers, or contractors.

P A R T

2

Commercial Real Estate Investment Types

17 **Single-Family Homes and Condominiums: A Great Place to Start**

18 **Apartment Complexes, Large and Small**

19 **Office Buildings**

20 **Retail Shopping Centers**

21 **Ministorage Facilities**

22 **Single-Tenant NNN Leased Investments**

23 **Land Brokerage**

24 **Mobile Home Parks**

17

Single-Family Homes and Condominiums:
A Great Place to Start

Many individuals enter the investment real estate market by acquiring single-family homes or condominiums. There are both advantages and disadvantages to starting with this type of investment.

Advantages

- *High leverage.* Today's real estate market has a multitude of lenders that will readily make 80 percent and even 90 percent loans on rental homes or condominiums. Few homes or condos will cash flow at 90 percent loan-to-value, so if the buyer wants to leverage that much, he or she will need to have a very high FICO score and ample cash reserves available. With low to moderate interest rates, most lower and midpriced homes and condos will break even at 75 to 80 percent loan-to-value ratios. When investing in condos, be careful to include the monthly homeowner's association (HOA) dues in your cash flow analysis, as some monthly HOA assessments are prohibitively high.

  If you are going to obtain financing in excess of 80 percent, get an 80 percent first loan and a lender fifteen-year second loan for the balance of the required financing. This will avoid having to pay for private mortgage insurance (PMI), which is not tax-deductible, and the rapid payoff of the second loan helps to build equity faster.

- *Rapid appreciation.* Single-family homes and condos tend to appreciate faster than other types of real estate investments, especially if you own one during one of the periods of ultrarapid housing inflation seen in the past several years.

Many investors have seen their equity double or triple in a year during these times. An investor who plans to acquire a home a year for three years in an area that has a history of high appreciation may very well find him- or herself in a position to trade up within five to six years to a small apartment house that will support professional management.

- *Large resale market.* The demand for resale homes and condos creates the largest real estate market in the United States. When it is time to dispose of the home as an investment, there is usually a large buyer pool ready to buy it if it is in good condition and priced appropriately. Be sure to offer the property to the tenant first when selling.

- *Ease of management.* Single-family homes and condos are usually easy to manage. The largest group of prospective tenants is usually families, and through careful screening you can usually get a tenant who will take reasonably good care of the property. As there is usually only one tenant, there is only one rent to collect and very few monthly bills to pay, so bookkeeping is easy. If you invest in a property near a college, then you may very well have multiple tenants and get higher-than-normal rents.

Disadvantages

- *Lack of cash flow.* Single-family homes and condos seldom produce enough rent to provide a meaningful cash flow unless the buyer pays 30 percent or more as down payment. The reduced leverage tends to lower the return on investment.

- *Potential higher vacancy rate.* Since there is usually only one tenant, the property is not bringing in any income if the tenant is not paying the rent or while it is vacant. There is no way to effectively "spread the risk" through multiple tenants.

- *Rent control.* Many cities and counties have rent control ordinances that must be identified *prior to* acquiring a residential income property, including rental homes and condominiums. Rent control can sharply limit the owner's ability to maintain a cash flow that is equal to or ahead of inflation.

- *Potential management issues.* Many excellent professional management firms are available that will take over complete rental and management duties of single-family homes and condos, usually for about 10 percent of collected rents. If you can't afford one of these firms, then you will be required to play landlord. This can be anything from a pleasant to a frightful experience. In 1973, I hired a young guy who started specializing in investment sales. He decided to manage the properties he sold. He came in one afternoon as white as a sheet and told me that a tenant had put a gun to his head when he knocked on the door and asked for the rent. He quickly decided to turn the property management duties over to other professionals.

> *He came in one afternoon as white as a sheet and told me that a tenant had put a gun to his head.*

You can sometimes end up with long-term tenants. This is good and bad. You avoid vacancies that way, but they often expect rent concessions in return, which can affect your cash flow. This won't affect the property's value as it would another type of income-producing property because the new buyer is usually not buying the property for its ability to produce income; they want a home to live in. A good way to handle a long-term tenant is to inform him or her you intend to raise the rent every year, but you will keep the rent a little below the going market rate for as long as the tenant stays. If tenants are told this right up front, they usually go along with it.

- *Maintenance.* Most condos are easy to maintain, as you only have to worry about the interior of the unit. The offset of this, of course, is the association dues you pay, which include reserves for roof replacement and other periodic structural maintenance that may not occur during your ownership. Single-family homes are a little different; they usually include lawns, shrubbery, and fences to maintain, as well as exterior and interior paint. Many tenants do not do a stellar job of maintaining homes the way an owner would. You need to be accepting of this, or it will drive you crazy. Think twice about buying a rental home with a swimming pool—it's probably not a good idea. If you do invest in one, rent it with pool service

> *Think twice about buying a rental home with a swimming pool.*

included. Renting a home with a gardener included is fairly easy to do; I've done so with some of the rentals I've owned over the years, and it has worked out fine. Accept the fact that when you sell the property, you will probably have to spend some money getting the property in shape.

- *Tenant issues when selling.* As I stated earlier, you will usually end up with a family or a single person as your tenant with this type of investment. They are never happy about receiving news from you that you are selling the property. It is not uncommon for the tenant to become uncooperative and make showing the property extremely difficult, if not impossible.

You have three choices:

1. You can wait out their lease and give them the required thirty-day notice to vacate, get them out, refurbish the property, and then market it vacant. Some properties show better when they are vacant; some show worse.
2. You can adhere to the terms of the lease and the landlord-tenant laws of your state and give them the required notice prior to each showing of the property. (This is very cumbersome and hard to do with an uncooperative tenant and sometimes leads to open confrontation.)
3. You can negotiate with the tenant and create a win-win situation. See the tenant personally to state your need to sell the property, and then offer a small rent concession of $75 to $200 a month off the rent. Tell the tenant that all showings will be by appointment only with a minimum two hours' notice unless the tenant is not home; then you will personally meet all agents and buyers wanting to see the property in the tenant's absence. Assure the tenant you will provide a minimum of forty-five days' notice before the tenant must vacate. (If you do this, be sure to construct the offer you receive to reflect the proper timing for the tenant's notice.) *Do not* put a keybox on the property as it violates the landlord-tenant act regulations requiring the landlord to give the required notice prior to showing the property. The notice period varies from state to state. California's is forty-eight hours, for example, while Arizona's is three days. Check your state and local ordinances.

18

Apartment Complexes, Large and Small

*W*hen talking about apartment complexes in this chapter, I will include everything from a duplex up to a large apartment complex with several hundred units. They all have a common theme: they provide shelter for people to live in and provide an income for the nonresident owner. In certain areas, they are also subject to rent control ordinances, so check your area's regulations carefully.

Smaller units, such as duplexes, triplexes, and four-unit buildings, are sometimes owner occupied and can provide the owner with a place to live and an income at the same time. The drawback to that arrangement is the tenants often feel that since the owner lives right there, it is all right to contact them at all hours and about the smallest issues. The owner's personality usually dictates how long he or she will endure that kind of intrusion before moving elsewhere or laying down the law to the tenants. This type of arrangement can be an excellent retirement planning vehicle for many people, and financing for two- to four-unit buildings is somewhat cheaper than for properties with five or more units.

Buildings containing five or more units are rarely owner occupied and are normally held for tax shelter and/or production of income. They can normally be financed to a maximum of 75 percent of their value and are not readily financed by lenders that finance owner-occupied one- to four-unit buildings. Builders sometimes build smaller units like this (from five to fifteen units) in pairs with a common driveway between them. If you, as an agent, ever list such a building, one of your first marketing activities should be to contact the owner of the building across the driveway to see if he or she would like to expand his or her holdings. Most often, these types of buildings have a recorded "mutual maintenance agreement" that calls for both owners to share maintenance and repairs of the driveway. It can be a source of irritation to an owner who maintains his or her property to share a driveway with an owner who doesn't; and if the "unmaintained" building is placed for sale, the owner across the driveway is often a motivated buyer. Most buildings of this size are nonamenity, with no swimming pool, recreation room, or exercise room, but there are a few exceptions.

Many states, including California, require a resident manager for buildings that contain sixteen units or more.

Buildings with about twenty to fifty units will very often have amenities such as swimming pools, recreation rooms, exercise rooms, and larger, comfortable lobbies where tenants can spend time. As these buildings start to become three-story, elevators become commonplace. This is a rather expensive additional operating cost, so be very careful to look into annual maintenance fees and repairs when you are doing an analysis of a building with an elevator or swimming pool. In many areas, it is common to see an apartment complex of several hundred units that is comprised of many twenty- to fifty-unit buildings. Due to the rising cost of homes, these types of buildings and complexes have been the favorite target of condominium conversion specialists.

> *Be very careful to look into annual maintenance fees and repairs when you are doing an analysis of a building with an elevator or swimming pool.*

Single buildings of about 60 to 150 units are considered midrise apartment complexes and are several stories high. Buildings of this size usually have a nice lobby and amenities such as pools, spas, and gymnasiums. They are also large enough to support a part-time or full-time maintenance staff. This may be one person or several, depending on the age, size, and condition of the building. These buildings are almost always managed by a professional property management company and have a resident manager.

Buildings over 150 units are generally in the high-rise category and contain many stories. Like the midrise buildings, they have a full-time support and maintenance staff, employ a resident manager, and are professionally managed. They, too, have a high degree of amenities. They are often located in urban downtown areas, and the first floor is usually retail shops and boutiques, while the second through third or fourth floors are often office space, with the remainder being residential apartments.

There is usually an inverse relationship between the location of an apartment complex and its capitalization rate: the better the location, the lower the cap rate. This means that an apartment complex in an old, declining area of town would sell at a higher cap rate than the same apartment complex would in a nicer area of town. It has to do with the risk/reward factor. Remember, a higher cap rate means a lower value, given the same net operating income, because you divide the net operating income by the cap rate to arrive at the property's value.

Apartment house brokerage is the area of commercial real estate where most agents work. It is the best understood area because of its similarities to residential home brokerage, and more agents are familiar with the landlord-tenant issues involved in apartment house sales than they are with other types of commercial real estate.

If you decide to specialize in apartment house brokerage of any size (and, yes, there is a very good living to be made in the smaller ones!), have your local title company get you a list of all of the ownership records in your area for the type or size units you are going to specialize in. There may be a small charge for this due to RESPA Section 8 restrictions. The list will have the site address, which is the address of the building you hope to market one day; it will also have the mailing address, which is the owner's mailing address. If the property is owned by an LLC, corporation, or other "holding entity," you will have to search CoStar, Loop Net, or the county records to get the name of an actual contact person. Get these contacts in your database, and start mailing and calling. Give it plenty of time; they need to get to know you before they will deal with

Use your title company as a resource—its staff are there to help.

you. This process applies to every type of commercial real estate product. Use your title company as a resource—its staff are there to help. Just be sure that you reward their efforts with some escrows.

19

Office Buildings

Office buildings come in a wide variety of shapes and sizes, from a home with commercial zoning that is converted to office use, to high-rise buildings like the Empire State Building.

Depending on your client's needs, a commercially zoned home on a main thoroughfare may be just perfect as it can afford a great deal of privacy and high visibility. Insurance brokers, mortgage brokers, chiropractors, dentists, and other small business owners tend to like the high visibility and easy access provided by this type of converted office space.

If you are representing a client in acquiring this type of space, you will need to be very careful about protecting their interests by looking into the current zoning as well as the need for any special use permits that may be required. A home with commercial zoning is not automatically granted a use permit for any type of business, so carefully assess your client's needs, and get him or her involved with the right people at the local planning and building departments. Be sure to include a contingency in any purchase offer you write for a client that says the sale is contingent on the property being approved for a use permit for the specific type of business he or she wants to open.

A drawback of owning this type of property is expansion. If your client plans on expanding the business, you should caution him or her to assess the size of the building being considered to see if it fits into any mid- or long-term expansion plans. Adding on additional space is expensive, and, depending on setback ordinances and other limiting factors, the building under consideration may prove to be too small or the floor plan not workable for the expansion your client has in mind.

Financing versus renting is also a consideration. When I owned my real estate company in the San Francisco Bay Area, I was strongly considering doing just what we have been talking about. In late 1979, I found a commercially zoned home in a very attractive location in town that was large enough to meet my business needs for several years to come. However, interest rates were climbing through the roof (they were about 12 percent at the time). When I looked into financing, I found that my monthly after-tax ownership costs didn't make the move from my current location attractive at all.

Many small office buildings have about 2,000 to 20,000 net-rentable square feet. A large number of these are privately owned, but many of the owners have formed a privately held LLC or corporation and have deeded the building to that entity for various tax- and liability-limiting purposes. If you subscribe to CoStar, you will be able to easily look up the name of a real person to communicate with; if not, you will need to do some digging through the county assessor's records to come up with a "person for service of notice." Every "nonhuman" form of property ownership, such as corporations, LLCs, Subchapter S corporations, and partnerships using a "doing business as" form (DBA), must file a form with the county recorder that tells the public who is empowered by that entity to be served papers for legal proceedings or other types of written communication. That will be your initial contact person.

These smaller office buildings have a wide variety of tenants that may include small real estate firms, mortgage brokerage firms, insurance brokers, and many other types of small businesses. The main advantage to the tenant of this type of office space instead of the converted home is the ability to expand without moving. My real estate company was in a neighborhood retail shopping center, and when the shoe store next door went out of business, I quickly took the space and expanded my operation.

The location of these types of office buildings varies widely, from marginal neighborhoods that are going through an economic downturn, to newly created neighborhoods that are thriving. The amount of rent charged will vary, depending on vacancy rates, the strength of the economy, and the prosperity of the area where the building is located.

While we are on the subject of rents, let's look at the various types of rent that can be charged for office space.

- *Gross lease.* In a gross lease, the tenant pays only the actual rent for the square feet his or her business occupies. Each unit will usually be separately metered for utilities, but the owner pays all other operating costs of the property.

- *Net lease.* In a net lease, the tenant pays the rent for the space occupied by his or her business as well as a proportional share of the real property taxes. The lease will usually include a clause that says the rent will increase proportionally as the property taxes do. Leases of three years or more usually have a "CPI (Consumer Price Index) increase" in them. This is a clause that increases the rent annually by an amount equal to the increase in the Consumer Price Index for that metropolitan area.

- *Net-net lease.* In a net-net lease, the tenant will usually be required to pay a proportional share of the insurance policy for the property as well as the real estate taxes. The same tax escalator and CPI increase clauses are usually found in these types of leases as well.

- *Net-net-net lease.* Often referred to as a NNN lease or "triple-net" lease, these leases state that the tenant pays a proportional share of all operating costs of the property, including real estate taxes, insurance, and maintenance and repairs. Most are specific about CAM, or common area maintenance, charges being paid by all tenants on a proportional basis that are usually tied to the percentage of square feet each tenant occupies compared with the total square feet of the building. With this type of lease, the owner pays no operating expenses at all; however, some leases of this nature include a charge for professional property management, and others do not. It is best to be very specific about this issue.

Although some office space is leased on a month-to-month basis or a one-year lease, most office space is leased for several years at a time. In order to stay even with the rate of inflation, these leases have built-in rental increases that are usually tied to the annual percentage rise in the CPI for a given metropolitan area, as stated earlier. You can find out what this figure is in your area by contacting your local Chamber of Commerce.

The age of the building will have an effect on the rents the owner can charge as well as on the operating expenses incurred by the owner, which may or may not be passed on to the tenants. Many, if not most, of these buildings have flat roofs coated with tar and gravel. It is important to build an annual fee into the operating budget of these buildings that allows for repairs each year and replacement about every twelve or so years (this will vary in different parts of the country).

Office buildings of this type can be vulnerable to a downturn in the economy and to business failures. A downturn in the economy will sometimes cause a marginally successful business to start to lose revenue. If the business owner does not have sufficient cash reserves and the business stops producing enough income to pay all of its operating expenses, including the rent, the owner may declare bankruptcy and go out of business, leaving the property owner with a nonpaying tenant or an extended vacancy. Owners of these types of office buildings are well advised to keep a reasonable cash reserve to cover loan payments and operating expenses in the event this happens. Generally, office buildings can only be financed to about 65 to 70 percent of their value, and because they are commercial, they are depreciated over thirty-nine years.

Owners of these types of office buildings are well advised to keep a reasonable cash reserve.

Many office buildings are in business parks. The entire park may be owned by one corporation, or each building may have an individual owner. If you are selling an office building in a business park, be careful to discover any association fees or other costs involved with ownership in the park as well as restrictions on signage.

As office buildings get larger, they tend to have lobbies and more amenities, much like apartment buildings. Many have conference rooms that can be reserved for use by the various businesses leasing space in them, and some have spas, gyms, boutiques, and retail centers on the ground floor.

Care must be taken when selling an office building to an investor when one tenant rents the majority of the space. You must carefully analyze that business's lease to see when it expires, what renewal options are available to the tenant in the lease, whether a renewal option has already been exercised before, and how well the business seems to be doing. If that tenant decides to vacate at the end of its lease, your investor could be faced with a mostly vacant building for an extended period of time.

Each new tenant in an office building will want tenant improvements (TIs) done to the space they are renting that are unique to their business. Who pays for these improvements is very negotiable and is usually dictated by demand for office space and the current state of the economy. In many cases, if the building owner pays for the TIs, the cost is amortized over the life of the initial lease period. The owner will always put a maximum limit on what tenants will pay, usually stated as a cost per net-rentable square foot. At times, office space has become overbuilt. When this happens, building owners will often give new tenants a certain number of months of free rent. This is also a very common incentive given to tenants who lease in new buildings, especially "name" tenants with strong financial backing from a Fortune 500 parent company.

Each new tenant in an office building will want tenant improvements (TIs) done to the space they are renting that are unique to their business.

20

Retail Shopping Centers

*R*etail shopping centers vary in size from the small strip center of a couple thousand square feet or the neighborhood shopping center with 80,000 to well over 100,000 square feet, to huge regional malls with over a million square feet or more. These properties are currently depreciated over a thirty-nine-year period.

The small strip center is very common in all urban areas and along major routes throughout the United States. The age of the building and the area where they are located usually dictate the amount and nature of rent owners are able to charge and the type of tenant they are able to attract.

An older strip center in a "B" area may only be able to generate gross leases because of the marginal type of tenants they are able to attract. These buildings are often occupied by pawn shops, ethnic markets, small cafés or restaurants, auto pink slip loan businesses, used book-stores, cellular phone companies, and other such businesses. The net profits derived from nearly all of these types of businesses often don't allow the business owner (tenant) to enter into NNN leases. Newer strip retail centers in better areas will often have real estate offices, in-surance brokers, opticians, franchise bagel or coffee stores, small restau-rants, and other tenants like those in office buildings. Their businesses will usually support the payment of a NNN lease, and those types of leases are much more prevalent in the better-located, newer strip retail centers.

Parking can often be marginal at best with strip centers, and, while many have ingress/egress easements with the neighboring properties, it is always good business to evaluate the effect of

It is always good business to evaluate the effect of available parking on the tenants' ability to attract customers.

available parking on the tenants' ability to attract customers. Real estate offices in these types of properties can sometimes be problematic as they need a great deal of parking for the sales agents and staff, which may not leave much for the customers and other tenants. If you help a client invest in a strip center or small neighborhood center that leases to a real estate firm, investigate what stipulations, if any, are in place to restrict where the sales agents may park.

Much like office buildings, free rent and payment of tenant improvements are inducements used to attract new retail tenants. The amount paid by owners, if any, is dictated by the supply-and-demand curve.

Strip centers are usually only financed to a maximum of 60 to 65 percent LTV ratio, and, because they are commercial in nature, the thirty-nine-year depreciation schedule must be used. Most leases in these centers are for an initial three- to five-year period and usually contain a renewal option for five years at a time.

Nearly every retail shopping center has cross-easements with the adjoining properties that allow customers to walk or drive from one center to the next without having to enter the roadway each time. Resurfacing of the parking lot is a major cost associated with a retail shopping center. If it is not done at reasonable intervals the pavement can start to split, get water under it, and begin to crumble. A "slurry coat" can be applied every few years accompanied by a restriping of the parking spots. (A slurry coat is a coat of liquid asphalt/tar that is sprayed over the existing asphalt to seal it from water penetration.) Some retail leases call for the tenants to pay into a parking lot maintenance fund. This money is supposed to be used to maintain the parking lot, but it is usually credited through escrow from one owner to the next and is only actually used when it is absolutely necessary.

Resurfacing of the parking lot is a major cost associated with a retail shopping center.

"Hydrocarbon" businesses are gas stations, oil-changing businesses, and any other businesses that use oil in any form. Hydrocarbon businesses are normally found in the neighborhood shopping centers and regional malls. It is rare that a strip center will have a business with hydrocarbons on site, but if you are involved in representing someone in the sale or purchase of a retail center that has hydrocarbons, be sure to see that a Phase 1 environmental report is ordered in a timely manner as this will certainly be a lender requirement if your investor is financing the acquisition. Three phases of environmental reports may apply to any property where hydrocarbons or other contaminants have been present:

- *Phase 1 environmental report.* This is a record check of the local building department, health department, or other government agency to see if there has been any cease and desist order made or any demand to clean up a hydrocarbon spill.

- *Phase 2 environmental report.* This is an on-site inspection of the business using hydrocarbons and the surrounding area to see if any visible spills or storage tank leakage has taken place.

- *Phase 3 environmental report.* This report requires boring test holes and obtaining soil samples at various spots around the affected property to see if any of the samples contain traces of hydrocarbons. Many lenders will make a Phase 2 environmental report a minimum requirement if there are any hydrocarbon businesses on the premises they are being asked to finance. If the property was ever foreclosed on by the lender, who then became the owner, that party could be made to pay for any environmental cleanup, which can cost from $300,000 to well over $1,000,000.

Like office buildings, retail shopping centers house businesses. That makes them and the tenants in them subject to the ups and downs of the economy, so when you are representing someone in the marketing or purchase of a retail shopping center, be sensitive to the current state of the national, state, and local economies, as all may affect the value of the property.

Neighborhood retail shopping centers are larger than strip centers and usually contain several acres of land. Many have an "anchor tenant" that adds value to the center because of its financial stability and its ability to attract customers to the center for the other businesses. Good examples of anchor tenants would be

Neighborhood retail shopping centers are larger than strip centers and usually contain several acres of land.

Costco, Wal-Mart, Safeway, Walgreens, or any other big-name commercial business. A center can also be "shadow anchored" by a major tenant; that is, the property immediately next to the center has a major tenant, and it is an easy walk to the "shadowed" retail center.

Neighborhood retail centers often have excellent restaurants, fast-food outlets, such as Burger King or McDonald's, and businesses that play to customers on a higher financial level. The larger ones are often anchored by an anchor tenant such as Home Depot, Lowe's, Costco, Target, or some other major retailer.

The regional malls are usually anchored by several major retailers such as JCPenney, Sears, Robinsons-May, Macy's, Banana Republic, or any number of other highly successful retailers. There are often several jewelry stores in a regional mall. One note of caution: there has been a movement of consolidation among some of the retailers in recent years, and if two or more major retail stores, such as Robinsons-May and Macy's (both are owned by Federated), are tenants in the same mall, the mall owners could be in for a vacancy if they combine operations, as just happened in the Tucson Mall in Tucson, Arizona.

Because of the large parking lots and security issues, the regional malls are more vulnerable to litigation from customers who have been assaulted or had their car stolen, so if you are involved in the brokerage of one of these malls, be sure to see what type of security patrols are in place, and check with the local law enforcement agencies to see what, if any, problems have occurred in the past two or three years.

Many of the leases signed by the major retailers are long term in nature, with many being for twenty-five to thirty years. An escalation clause related to the CPI is almost always in place, usually with a cap of 5 to 7 percent annually. These types of leases are very lengthy and detailed, and they should always be reviewed by the buyer's attorney and CPA. Most neighborhood retail centers and all regional malls have leases that allow the major tenants a rent abatement or the right to abandon their lease in the event another major tenant leaves the premises.

21

Ministorage Facilities

*M*inistorage, or self-storage facilities, as they are often called, are a very different breed of real estate investment. Not the sexiest income-producing properties by any means, but properly managed, they are unequaled as cash cows! Ministorage facilities have a true operating expense ratio of about 19 percent of gross scheduled income, as compared with 30 to 36 percent for apartment houses.

Not the sexiest income-producing properties by any means, but properly managed, they are unequaled as cash cows!

Ministorage facilities can consist of a small plot of land with fewer than thirty units to several acres containing several hundred units with two-story air-conditioned buildings. They are often located near mobile home parks and large residential subdivisions as these are target tenants due to a need for additional storage. Many facilities derive additional income from truck or trailer rentals and the sale of moving boxes and related goods. Some facilities are a combination of ministorage and boat/RV storage.

There are three main types of construction of ministorage facilities: concrete block walls with sloped tar and gravel roofs and metal doors, all-metal construction, and wood frame/stucco with a hip roof.

Regardless of the type of construction, care must be taken to evaluate the soil prior to construction. Heavy clay soil expands when it gets wet, and if the facility's foundation preparation is not done properly, every time it rains the soil under the units expands unevenly, and the garage entry doors to the units won't open because the door tracks are thrown out of alignment. You may avoid this problem by constructing "floating foundations" where the perimeter foundation is poured, and then about two feet of soil is removed from the interior and replaced with gravel and nonexpansive dirt that is compacted to 94 percent. A floating foundation is poured over the compacted nonexpansive soil, and the buildings are then built on the floating foundation, which rises and falls evenly.

Concrete block construction is labor-intensive to build but easily maintained thereafter. Most concrete block facilities have sloped tar and gravel roofs that need to be maintained on a regular basis. When doing an income/expense analysis on this type of facility, be sure to allow for annual maintenance fees and a reserve fund to allow for roof replacement at regular intervals of about ten to fifteen years, depending on where the facility is located.

Metal buildings are the least expensive to construct, but they can be more of a maintenance challenge, depending on the type and quality of construction. For instance, they usually have pitched metal roofs that are fastened together with rivets at the roof apex. To avoid leaking, plastic grommets are used in conjunction with the rivet installation. If the roof apex is not protected from the elements, the sun will eventually cause the grommets to become so brittle that they will crack and come apart, causing massive roof leaks. Replacing them can be a maintenance nightmare. In better-quality metal construction, a metal cap that runs the entire length of each building is placed over the rivets and snapped in place. This cap acts as a barrier from both sun and water and effectively solves the leak situation. Not all types of metal construction can be retrofitted with a cap system, so be sure to investigate this issue during your due diligence period if you are representing a buyer for this type of construction.

Wood frame/stucco construction with a normal hip roof that slopes down on each side has become very popular in the last twenty years. It is easy to construct and reasonably easy to maintain. Your exterior maintenance reserves will be for painting and roof replacement every so often, but the roof type is usually much more adaptable than tar and gravel and will not have to be done as often. This type of construction is very often found in two-story facilities. A two-story facility will, out of necessity, include an elevator. Elevator maintenance will increase your operating expenses somewhat, so be careful to check on elevator maintenance costs in your area.

Up until about 1980, the main type of security at a ministorage facility was when the resident manager closed and locked the gate at night and let the guard dogs out. Theft deterrence and security has become an issue with ministorage facilities, and closed-circuit television systems that monitor an entire facility are routine now. All but the smallest facilities have an on-site apartment where a resident manager lives. The ideal candidate for this position is often a retired husband-wife team who get free rent and a salary in return for overseeing the operation. They act as night guards and run the day-to-day operation, which includes collecting rents, showing and renting units, handling notices and on-site auctions of personal property left by people who don't pay or abandon property on the site, and doing some level of recordkeeping and banking.

Ministorage facilities have often been constructed on land purchased by a developer who wants to derive an income from the property while he or she waits for the urban spread to reach the property, making it much more valuable for residential development.

Location is extremely important when considering a ministorage acquisition or new-build. You must be certain that the site location is not vulnerable to someone building a new facility nearer to your target market than your site is, because this may cause many of your tenants to vacate and move to it, and your target market will probably opt to rent at the newer, closer facility.

You must be certain that the site location is not vulnerable to someone building a new facility nearer to your target market than your site is.

If you ever want to spend a couple of days in the company of a large group of very low-key multimillionaires, attend the annual ministorage owners' convention. They are a very impressive group!

Ministorage developments are also depreciated over a thirty-nine-year period.

Single-Tenant NNN Leased Investments

*T*hese types of investments are often called "coupon clippers," because the owner has virtually no management duties or obligations except to cash the rent check. These investments include

These types of investments are often called "coupon clippers."

fast-food restaurants such as McDonald's and Burger King, auto care firms such as Midas Muffler shops and Jiffy Lube, Walgreens and other major drug stores, bank branch offices, major supermarkets such as Safeway, and major chain retailers such as Target, PetSmart, K-Mart and others. Many of the larger types of these investments are anchor tenants in large neighborhood shopping centers, while some, such as the drug stores and banks, may be stand-alone.

The tenant pays virtually all operating costs incurred in connection with the property, and the rent is usually paid or guaranteed by the parent company, which is often a Fortune 500 company or very successful owner of a regional franchise.

The leases are usually for a longer period of time—some as long as twenty-five to thirty years. Because of the longer term, the lease almost always contains an escalator clause that adjusts the rent period-ically to keep up with inflation. The increases are usually tied to the Cost of Living Index (CPI) and most are "capped" at 5 to 7 percent annually.

There is a tax issue with NNN leased investments that you should al-ways have your client investigate with their CPA or tax attorney prior to making this type of investment. Because the owner has virtually no ongoing management duties and doesn't meet the 750-hour annual rule, they may not eligible to take a depreciation allowance from the property.

When helping a client invest in these types of properties, you need to do several things as part of your due diligence.

- *Carefully review the lease.*

    1. How much time is remaining on the lease?
    2. Are there any options to renew?
    3. How likely is it they will renew?
    4. Is there a CPI escalator clause?
    5. Is it a true NNN lease?
    6. Is there a major net worth guarantor on the lease?
    7. Who pays for roof and parking lot maintenance?

- *What is the condition and status of the area?*

    1. Is the area building, static, or in decline? If, for instance, you are showing your client a supermarket that is in the last six years of a thirty-year lease in an older retail center, and a new center is being built a few blocks away that will include a major competitor supermarket, the tenant in the property you are showing to your client may be considering closing that operation at the end of the current lease. That would leave your client with the possibility of a huge loan payment and no income to pay it.
    2. What is the crime rate in the area?
    3. Is the area experiencing growth, maturity, or is it in a state of decline?

- *What is the condition of the building and the retail center it is in, if applicable?*

    1. While it is true the tenant must maintain the building, what kind of a job are they doing?
    2. Is there any sign of deferred maintenance?
    3. Does the property have any functional obsolescence that would be very expensive or impossible to cure?
    4. If the property is in a retail center, how well is the center being maintained?

If the property is in a retail center, how well is the center being maintained?

23

Land Brokerage

*L*and brokerage has one of the highest litigation rates against brokers of any type of commercial brokerage. It is no place for the unschooled to dally, and it is one of the most scrutinized areas of commercial brokerage by the Department of Real Estate.

Land brokerage has one of the highest litigation rates against brokers of any type of commercial brokerage.

Land brokerage includes selling subdivided lots in existing subdivisions where homes have already been built, newly subdivided lots that are being sold to the public or to builders by a developer, the sale of larger estate-type acreage to custom home builders or homeowners, and the sale of raw land to developers. The sale of ranches and farms is somewhat different as it also entails the sale of an existing business with the land. Ranch and farm brokerage is an even more specialized type of land sales and should only be conducted by highly experienced professionals.

Let's take a look at each one.

Subdivided Lots in Existing Subdivisions

This is the safest type of land sale, especially if there are already several homes built around the lot you are trying to sell. The reasons it is safer are as follows:

- It is easier to verify the existence and exact location of all utilities, including natural gas, electricity, water, and trash removal.

- It is easier to verify the existence of sewer lines and hookup capability, or to obtain existing percolation tests of adjoining properties, if an on-site waste treatment system such as a septic system is needed.

- Boundary lines are easier to determine.

- The existence of any flood zones or special study zones, such as seismic study zones or earthquake zones in California, are easier to determine.

- The availability of, and who is responsible for, crime and fire prevention is easier to determine.

- There are often more recent comparable sales to use in determining the property value.

- Is this the first sale of this property to the public? If so, a Final Public Report may be needed.

Newly Subdivided Land Being Sold to the Public or to Builders

This type of land brokerage gets into the use and proper issuance of many items not used in resale land brokerage. Some of these are as follows:

- *A Commissioner's Preliminary Subdivision Public Report.* In most states, a developer can take a reservation on a lot from the public and can take a refundable deposit. The buyer must acknowledge receipt of a Preliminary Public Report, and the reservation is cancelable by either party until the buyer is issued a Final Public Report, at which time the sale is finalized and the buyer's deposit becomes nonrefundable.

- *A Final Subdivision Public Report.* Once a subdivision is fully approved by the Department of Real Estate, a Final Public Report will be issued. Anyone who entered into a reservation must either sign for the Final Public Report and make the deposit

> *Once a subdivision is fully approved by the Department of Real Estate, a Final Public Report will be issued.*

nonrefundable at that time, or withdraw from the reservation and receive their deposit back. All new sales are binding at that time and must include the buyer's signed receipt for the Final Public Report.

- *Rights of rescission time limits.* Land subdivisions are often subject to longer and more stringent time periods for the buyers to reconsider and cancel the purchase. California, for instance, has a ten-day right of rescission for new subdivision land sales.

- *Trust fund handling of customer deposits.* It is common for a developer to have language in the purchase agreement he or she is using that alerts the buyer that the developer is placing the buyer's deposit into the developer's business account and not into a neutral escrow account. This could place the buyer's deposit in jeopardy if the developer files for bankruptcy protection.

- *Due diligence periods (also called feasibility study periods).* Builders who purchase lots in bulk from a subdivider almost always want a "feasibility study" or "due diligence" period included in their purchase or option agreement. The timing of these periods can vary from a few weeks to several months and allows the builder/buyer time to assess the strength or weakness of the current market and the anticipated market conditions when he or she is able to bring a finished home to the market. Your job as an agent for the builder would be to obtain information about what price range home would be optimal to build on the land the builder is acquiring and what the anticipated absorption rate would be (how fast the builder's product would be purchased by the public).

As the agent for the developer, your job would be to get as high a price per lot from the builders and individual buyers as possible with the fewest concessions possible. You may be asked to help the developer determine the optimum lot premium that should be charged for each lot in the subdivision he or she is developing. You may also be asked to plan a complete marketing and advertising campaign, including newsprint, websites, marketing brochures, and direct mailing campaigns.

The developer often relies on his or her real estate agent to obtain comparable sales information of similar land transactions so that the developer can properly plan his or her best pricing strategy and optimize his or her profit from the venture.

The developer often relies on his or her real estate agent to obtain comparable sales information of similar land transactions.

The Sale of Larger Estate-Type Acreage to Custom Home Builders or Homeowners

This type of sale can often be done in such a manner that the issuance of a Final Commissioner's Public Report is not needed. You must be careful to see that any subdivision of land in this manner is a legitimate one and not a "wildcat" subdivision as defined by the Department of Real Estate in your state. For instance, in Arizona, any land subdivision of five or fewer parcels is exempt from a public report, while California's threshold is six or fewer parcels. Commissioner's Preliminary and Final Public Reports take a lot of time and cost a lot of money, so some developers are tempted to do a wildcat subdivision to avoid the time and expense.

I was recently made aware of a situation where a newer agent was listing a man's ten-acre parcel that he had subdivided into five two-acre parcels. The agent was walking the property with the seller and an appraiser and met the owner of the adjacent ten-acre parcel, which he had just acquired as well. She asked him if he would consider selling his five two-acre parcels, and he agreed. When the listings were reviewed by the branch manager, he became suspicious and investigated further, at which time he found that this was, indeed, a wildcat subdivision of a twenty-acre parcel that was split into two ten-acre parcels and then resplit into five two-acre parcels each. He cancelled the listing and notified the Department of Real Estate, as he was supposed to do.

The Department of Real Estate levied a heavy fine against each property owner and issued a cease-and-desist order, stopping the sale, and it notified both owners that they could not sell the land for at least two years. The designated broker of the firm was fined $4,000 because the agent took the listings; the branch manager was fined $2,000 because the agent took the listings; the agent was fined $20,000 and almost had her license suspended. As you can see, it is easy to become entangled in something very unpleasant if you are not familiar with what you are doing in land sales.

Your job as a builder's representative is to help assess the value of each parcel acquired by your builder client and the optimum price, style, and size home that can be built on each one. An assessment of the current market and the anticipated strength or weakness of the market when the finished home is placed for sale are also among your duties. This price analysis is critical to the success of the project as it allows the builder or developer to maximize profits by not overpaying for the land.

Some builders of these types of homes will rely heavily on their agents for staging and decorating advice; others will use the services of a professional decorator, especially if model homes are involved.

Sale of Raw Land to Developers

This area of land sales probably has the highest legal exposure for a real estate professional. This is where you, as an agent, are finding and presenting large parcels of undeveloped land to developers and builders.

Many issues need to be investigated during the due diligence period. Some states maintain that you, as the agent for the developer, are primarily responsible for proper investigation of material facts regarding the proposed land purchase on behalf of your client. Some states maintain that the client is primarily responsible for the investigation of material facts, and as the agent, you are secondarily responsible. Either way, you will need to become keenly aware of any land-related issues that could affect the proposed purchase your client is about to make. Zoning, special-study (earthquake) zones, flood zones, known "brownfields" or areas of contamination, building height or size restrictions, minimum lot size issues, building setback ordinances, and sewer capacity availability are just a few of the issues you will need to be aware of. Failure to investigate even one of these can result in your client purchasing land that he or she cannot develop as planned, and your client could take a huge loss or lose a large earnest money deposit.

Failure to investigate even one of these can result in your client purchasing land that he or she cannot develop as planned.

Arizona places the primary responsibility on the client but holds the agent to a high degree of backup responsibility. A case happened just recently where a developer-client made an offer to purchase over 130 acres for residential development. He was very egotistical, and when the agent reminded him to check on the sewer capacity, he told the agent that he knew what he was doing and had a whole team to do that stuff. Fortunately, the agent faxed the developer the paperwork to fill out and submit to the county to find out about sewer capacity. The client initialed each page and faxed it back. Well after the expiration of the due diligence period, the developer became aware that there was *no* sewer capacity, and he cancelled the sale. He threatened to sue the agent, broker, and seller for "willful nondisclosure" and fraud if his $50,000 deposit was not returned. When his attorney was presented with the county paperwork that was sent to and initialed by him, he redirected his wrath at the seller for failure to disclose the lack of sewer capacity (the seller knew it and didn't disclose it), and he got his deposit back. Having "provable" evidence of diligence on the agent's part by faxing the paperwork and getting it back saved the agent and brokerage firm many thousands of dollars in defense fees.

Anyone who is sincerely interested in specializing in land brokerage is well advised to start taking course offerings in land sales. The REALTORS® Land Institute offers a course of study leading to the RLI professional designation.

24

Mobile Home Parks

Mobile home parks may consist of a couple of acres to several acres of land that have been developed with streets that have cement pads on either side to accommodate mobile homes. The mobile homes may be either park owned and rented to tenants, or tenant owned, and the tenant pays a space rental for the pad and surrounding area they rent. Mobile home parks can usually be financed to about 60 to 65 percent of appraised value.

Most mobile home parks have amenities available for use by the tenants. The amount and type of amenities will usually vary according to the economic stature of the community and neighborhood they are located in and may include a swimming pool, clubhouse, exercise room, or vending machines.

> *The amount and type of amenities will usually vary according to the economic stature of the community and neighborhood they are located in.*

Mobile home parks have varying levels of quality. Some of the factors that define the quality of a mobile home park are described here.

The Ratio of Single-Wide to Double-Wide Units

A mobile home park that has many or mostly single-wide units will usually have a higher vacancy rate than a park that has all or mostly double-wide units. The reason is that the owner of a single-wide unit can easily hook it up to a truck or SUV and move it to another park, leaving the park owner with a vacant pad, while the owner of a double-wide unit must have the unit split in two and hauled to another location on two flatbed trucks followed by a vehicle bearing a "Wide Load" sign behind them. This is expensive to do, so if the owner of a double-wide mobile home wishes to move, he or she will almost always sell the unit and purchase a new one at the new destination. The effect of this on the park owner is that the space is always rented.

Location

Parks that are mostly or totally single-wide in nature are most often found in areas that are on the lower end of the socioeconomic scale in any given community because they afford relatively inexpensive shelter. Parks that tend to have mostly or all double-wide units are usually found in more upscale areas of a community. There are many parks across the country that are absolutely beautiful, with a large number of amenities and long-term tenants. The capitalization rate for a park of this nature will be lower (meaning a higher relative value) than for a mostly single-wide park.

Amenities

While there are few, if any, amenities in a single-wide park because the tenants aren't seeking them, they become an important drawing card for tenants in double-wide parks because these individuals are often retired and are looking for social interaction with other people to fill their time. A central clubhouse, swimming pool, and spa or exercise room are all sought-after features.

Condition of Park-Owned Units

If you, as an agent, are representing an investor in the purchase of a mobile home park, you should advise the client to have the condition of any park-owned units checked thoroughly by an inspector who is familiar with mobile home construction. The inspector must be especially diligent in checking the plumbing because many mobile homes built in the 1980s and early 1990s were constructed with polybutylene plastic plumbing that is *very* prone to cracking at the joints and leaking.

You should advise the client to have the condition of any park-owned units checked thoroughly by an inspector who is familiar with mobile home construction.

Off-Site Issues

In evaluating a mobile home park, you should be careful to look over the entire property. Ask or do the following:

1. Are the streets and common areas maintained properly?

    - Are roads properly surfaced and free of ruts, dips, and cracks?
    - Are the lawns mowed and trimmed?
    - Are the common buildings painted and in good repair?
    - Is the pool and spa maintained properly, and are there child safety barriers in place?
    - Are the units required to have skirts and be on blocks or jacks?
    - Are the lots wide enough to accommodate a carport?
    - What security measures are in place for the park?
    - What is the park's proximity to shopping, schools, public transportation, and medical facilities?

2. Meet the on-site managers. Interview them; look over their quarters, if possible.

    - Are they neat and orderly?
    - Do they seem sharp and in touch with what is going on around the park?
    - If you see any deferred maintenance, ask the managers about why it exists. An interview of this type will tell you much about how well run the park is.

3. Do a thorough review of the park owner's accounting records for the past two years. Pay special attention to the following:

    - Total income.

        a. What was the total income received from all sources during the past two years and year to date?
        b. Does the income show a seasonal trend? Some parks have tenancies that are seasonal in nature. If this is the case, your investor needs to know that he or she will need to use excess reserves carefully to see the operation through the "off-season."

- Total expenses.

    a. Look for any excessive or unusual expenses. Ask what they were for or why they were made if the reason is not clear. Many income property owners pay themselves "perks" for tax reasons that need to be added back into income as they are personal in nature, such as car payments, travel, and other items.

    b. Compare the property taxes for the two years to see how much the annual increase was, if any.

    c. Look for a pattern of routine maintenance expenditures, for both the rental units and the general buildings and area maintenance. This would include painting, lawn and garden care, tree trimming, road maintenance, janitorial services and/or supplies, and pool/spa maintenance and supplies.

    d. Calculate the vacancy factor, both in dollars and as a percentage of gross rents. See if it matches any marketing brochure you have received.

Appendices

Appendix 1

Sample Annual Property Operating Data (APOD)

Annual Property Operating Data

Property Name _____
Location _____
Type of Property _____
Size of Property _____ (sf/Units)

Purpose of Analysis _____

Assessed/Appraised Values
Land _____ _____
Improvements _____ _____
Personal Property _____ _____
Total _____ _____

Adjusted Basis as of _____

Purchase Price _____
Plus Acquisition Costs _____
Plus Loan Fees/Costs _____
Less Mortgages _____
Equals Initial Investment _____

	Balance	Periodic Payment	Pmts/ Yr	Interest	Amort Period	Loan Term
1st						
2nd						

	ALL FIGURES ARE ANNUAL	$/sf or $/Unit	% of GOI	COMMENTS/FOOTNOTES
1	POTENTIAL RENTAL INCOME			
2	Less: Vacancy & Cr. Losses	(_____ % of PRI)		
3	EFFECTIVE RENTAL INCOME			
4	Plus: Other Income (Collectable)			
5	GROSS OPERATING INCOME			
6	OPERATING EXPENSES:			
7	Real Estate Taxes			
8	Personal Property Taxes			
9	Property Insurance			
10	Off Site Management			
11	Payroll			
12	Expenses/Benefits			
13	Taxes/Workers' Compensation			
14	Repairs and Maintenance			
	Utilities:			
15	_____			
16	_____			
17	_____			
18	_____			
19	Accounting and Legal			
20	Licenses/Permits			
21	Advertising			
22	Supplies			
23	Miscellaneous Contract Services:			
24	_____			
25	_____			
26	_____			
27	_____			
28	_____			
29	TOTAL OPERATING EXPENSES			
30	NET OPERATING INCOME			
31	Less: Annual Debt Service			
32	Less: Participation Payments			
33	Less: Leasing Commissions			
34	Less: Funded Reserves			
35	CASH FLOW BEFORE TAXES			

Prepared for: _____
Prepared by: _____

Sample Letter of Intent (LOI)

SKYLINE DEVELOPMENT CO., LLC
11165 N. La Canada Drive, Suite 175, Oro Valley, Arizona 85737
Office: 520.555.2403
Fax: 520.555.8837

December 11, 2007
Mr. Barry Edwards;
Tucson, Arizona

RE: Sale of approximately ±147.32 acres of vacant land, Pima County Assessor's #831-92-300B, 8160,8260,8360 (the "**Property**")

Dear Mr. Edwards:

The purpose of this letter is to indicate the basis upon which Mr. Barry Edwards (the "**Seller**") is prepared to proceed with the sale of the Property, subject to the completion and execution of a definitive written purchase and sale agreement satisfactory to both parties and their respective counsel.

PROPERTY:	Vacant land containing approximately 147.32 acres in Tucson, Arizona, and controlled by Pima County
PURCHASER:	Skyline Development Co., LLC, an Arizona limited liability company (the "**Purchaser**")
PURCHASE PRICE:	Two Million Eight Hundred Thousand Dollars and no Cents ($2,800,000.00); or Three Million Three Hundred Fifty Two Thousand Dollars and no Cents ($3,352,000) if seller agrees to a Fifty % carryback at 7.5% for a period not to exceed Fourteen Months. Seller shall be

---

Sample Letter of Intent, continued

<table>
<tr>
<td></td>
<td>paid interest payments quarterly and purchaser reserves the right to prepay the entire principal balance at any time without penalty.</td>
</tr>
<tr>
<td>EARNEST MONEY:</td>
<td>Purchaser shall deposit Thirty Five Thousand Dollars ($35,000.00) into escrow with the escrow agent defined below within 48 hours after the execution of the Purchase Agreement. Upon expiration of the due diligence period, Purchaser shall deposit an additional Sixty-Five Thousand Dollars ($65,000.00) for a total of One Hundred Thousand Dollars and no Cents ($100,000.00). Earnest money shall be deposited with Title Security Agency, Inc., 6970 N. Oracle Road, Suite 201, Tucson, Arizona 85704, (520) 555-1212, and to the attention of Mrs. Elaine Johnson (the "Escrow Agent"). Earnest money shall become non-refundable at the end of the due diligence period, unless the purchase and sale contract is appropriately terminated by Purchaser. All monies shall be used as part of the down payment.</td>
</tr>
<tr>
<td>DUE DILIGENCE PERIOD:</td>
<td>Sixty days (60) days from full execution of the Purchase Agreement by both parties.</td>
</tr>
<tr>
<td>DUE DILIGENCE REPORTS:</td>
<td>All due diligence studies and reports shall be the responsibility of Purchaser and at Purchaser's expense. All</td>
</tr>
</table>

Sample Letter of Intent, continued

administration concerning the Property, not limited to and to include Alta survey, topographical within a 2 ft contour, engineering and hydrological data, site assessment and biological impact data shall be released in digital format from Seller or Seller's agents to Purchaser or to Purchaser's agents and are to be made immediately upon mutual Purchase Agreement execution and available to Seller.

PURCHASER'S INVESTIGATION RIGHTS:

The Property is being sold "AS IS" without warranty or representation as to its physical condition, compliance with current codes or fitness for a particular purpose. At Purchaser's sole discretion, Purchaser or its authorized representatives shall be entitled to enter upon the Property and make such surveying, engineering, physical, and other studies as Purchaser deems fit. Prior to any such entry upon the Property, Purchaser shall sign a right of entry and nondisclosure agreement, provide notice to Seller of its intended scope of work and Purchaser shall indemnify Seller as to its actions and its authorized representative's and contractor's actions on the Property, during the performance of the investigation.

Purchaser may perform an environmental Phase I study on the Property. However,

Sample Letter of Intent, continued

should a Phase II be desired, Purchaser must obtain Seller's agreement on the scope of the work and obtain Seller's written approval.

After all such investigation, if Purchaser in its sole discretion determines that the Property is not satisfactory to Purchaser, then Purchaser may terminate the transaction by notifying Seller in writing no later than the end of the due diligence period.

TITLE & SURVEY: Seller shall convey its fee simple interest in the Property by a special warranty deed subject to items of record.

CLOSING: Property will be placed in escrow upon full execution of the purchase and sale agreement and closing will occur at the expiration of Forty-Five (45) days from date of the successful completion of the due diligence period.

CLOSING COSTS: Seller shall pay for the owner's title insurance policy, extended coverage, and all endorsements. Purchaser shall pay for the cost of any survey, if necessary. Purchaser shall pay for the costs incurred in connection with its physical inspection of the Property. Other normal costs associated with the closing, including recording fees, escrow fees, and transfer taxes, shall be paid and split according to local custom and practice in the local market. The purchase price shall

Sample Letter of Intent, continued

	be adjusted in accordance with generally accepted accounting principles for real estate taxes, credits, and other adjustments.
BROKERAGE COMMISSION:	The parties represent and warrant that Herd Realty Corporation and Sunshine Realty Company, Inc., will be paid a 6% commission, 3% each to the listing and sales office for a real estate broker's commission.
CONTRACT:	Upon execution of this letter by both parties, Purchaser will draft the proposed purchase and sale agreement, which shall be submitted to Seller for review and comment. Both parties agree to employ the appropriate resources to use reasonable efforts to execute a purchase and sale agreement within Fifteen (15) business days after Seller's receipt of this LOI.
BACKUP BUYER:	Purchaser acknowledges that prior to closing, Seller may negotiate a sale of the Property to another entity (the "Backup Buyer"), pursuant to a contract, letter of understanding, other writing, or oral agreement. The rights of the Backup Buyer with respect to the Property will expire upon the closing herein. If Purchaser and Seller negotiate, execute, and deliver a purchase and sale contract with respect to the Property that is subsequently terminated, then Seller may sell the Property to the Backup

Sample Letter of Intent, continued

Buyer or any other buyer at any time free and clear of any claim of Purchaser. Purchaser will render reasonable cooperation prior to closing hereunder to permit the Backup Buyer to concurrently perform its due diligence investigation at no cost to Purchaser and so long as the Backup Buyer does not interfere with Purchaser's due diligence investigation.

CONFIDENTIALITY: Seller and Purchaser shall keep all information and reports obtained from Seller relating to the Property or the proposed transaction confidential and will not disclose any such confidential information to any other person or entity without obtaining the prior written consent of Seller and Purchaser. If a purchase and sale agreement is executed by the parties, Purchaser and Seller shall keep all terms of the purchase and sale agreement confidential and may disclose only such terms as are necessary to each party's attorneys, accountants, and other professional advisors.

ANNOUNCEMENTS: Seller and Purchaser shall consult with each other in advance with regard to all press releases and other announcements issued concerning this transaction or the transactions contemplated hereby and, except as may be required by applicable laws or the applicable rules and regulations of any governmental agency,

Sample Letter of Intent, continued

	neither Seller nor Purchaser shall issue any press release, Internet article or other such publicity without the prior written consent of the other party, which consent may be granted or withheld in the consenting party's sole discretion.
REMEDIES:	The terms of the Purchase and Sale Agreement and escrow instructions shall govern remedies in the event either party terminates the purchase and sale contract or cancels escrow.
APPROVAL:	This transaction is expressly contingent upon obtaining a review and approval from Purchaser's legal counsel regarding the subsequent executed Purchase Agreement and written approval thereof during the due diligence period.
NONBINDING AGREEMENT:	Other than the confidentiality provisions of Section 14 herein, this letter is a **nonbinding** proposal and no party shall have the right to institute any legal actions with respect to the transaction described herein.

Seller and Purchaser acknowledge that this nonbinding proposal is not an offer, and that it is intended only as the basis for setting forth general terms and conditions and for further negotiation for the Property described herein. Either party can terminate negotiations at any time without any liability to the other party and neither party shall have any obligation to negotiate in good faith. The parties acknowledge that the terms contained herein do not include all of the material terms and conditions which would be required in a definitive agreement. Both

Sample Letter of Intent, continued

parties agree that only a final agreement containing all of the terms required by both Purchaser and Seller, executed by each party and placed in escrow, will constitute a binding agreement for a purchase of the Property, subject to the rights of other parties. Seller has until 5:00 P.M., Mountain Standard Time, on November 30, 2007, to provide a written response to this Letter of Intent.

AGREED AND ACCEPTED AND ACKNOWLEDGED THIS _____ DAY OF November, 2007:

SELLER: PURCHASER:
By: Skyline Development Co., LLC

_____   _____

By: Mr. Barry Edwards   By: William Claussen, Managing Partner

_____   _____

By: By:

About the Author

Bob Herd started his real estate career in early 1972 with a small real estate company on the San Francisco Peninsula.

Although no formal training programs or systems were available in those days, Bob used some good initial training from his branch manager, his natural ability to interact with people, and his keen intuition about human nature to sell more than sixty homes in his first and second years in the business. He was awarded the coveted "Top Salesperson" award from the real estate association that he belonged to in 1974.

Bob's wife Eileen was licensed in 1975 and became his licensed assistant on a part-time basis until their four children were grown; she then became his full-time assistant. Her help was very instrumental in his receipt of the "Top Salesperson" award and his continuing success throughout his career in sales.

Although Bob opened his own highly successful company in 1974, he still remained very active in sales, and under his training and guidance, one of his agents won the "Top Salesperson" award from the same association every year for the next six years, except for 1979.

Over the course of his career, which spans more than thirty-two years, Bob has been a salesperson, broker/owner, branch manager, and regional manager for some of the largest real estate companies in the San Francisco Bay Area and Tucson, Arizona. Whether he was in a sales position or a nonselling management position, he always maintained and nurtured in his associates a keen sense of the ever-evolving sensible, human-nature-based style of professionally handling the needs of customers and clients and the far-reaching effectiveness of working with a top licensed assistant.

Bob maintains both a California and an Arizona broker's license and holds the Certified Residential Brokerage Manager (CRB), Certified Residential Specialist (CRS), and Graduate, Realtors Institute (GRI) designations. He is currently a branch manager for Coldwell Banker Success Southwest in Tucson, Arizona. You may reach Bob at (520) 240-2403 or by e-mail at rlherd@comcast.net.

Index